Immortal
speeches

Compiled by
Harshvardhan Dutta

UNICORN BOOKS

Publishers
UNICORN BOOKS Pvt. Ltd. Delhi

E-mail: unicornbooks@vsnl.com • *Website:* www.unicornbooks.in
©Copyright : Unicorn Books Pvt. Ltd.

Distributors
Pustak Mahal, Delhi-110006

J-3/16 , Daryaganj, New Delhi-110002
☎ 23276539, 23272783, 23272784 • *Fax:* 011-23260518
E-mail: info@pustakmahal.com • *Website:* www.pustakmahal.com

Branch Offices
Bangalore: ☎ 22234025
E-mail: pmblr@sancharnet.in • pustak@sancharnet.in
Mumbai: ☎ 22010941
E-mail: rapidex@bom5.vsnl.net.in
Patna: ☎ 3094193 • *Telefax:* 0612-2302719
E-mail: rapidexptn@rediffmail.com
Hyderabad: *Telefax:* 040-24737290
E-mail: pustakmahalhyd@yahoo.co.in

ISBN 81-780-6093-0

Contents

History of Oratory

The history of speeches is deeply associated with ancient Greece and Rome. It is believed that the ancient Greeks and Romans were great orators and used speeches effectively, in times of peace or war, to inspire their men. The plays of ancient Greeks were filled with inspirational speeches that even inspired the audiences. The protagonist of the 'Iliad' Achilles is widely known for the eloquent speeches he has made in the epic.

The pioneer of the art of oratory is believed to be Corax, a Greek lawyer in the 5th century B.C., who wrote a book named 'Principles of Forensic Oratory'. This book is still considered the basis of all forensic speeches. The book states that all legal matters have a certain structure. He gives the following principles for good speeches:

- The opening of the speech should create the right mood and tell the audience what the speech will be all about.
- The speech should state the facts of the case clearly and
- the speaker should draw out the inferences made from the facts.
- He should fasten up the loose ends and
- the ending of the speech should be convincing and persuasive.

Demosthenes: When the legal disputes in the country grew, the speechmakers formed themselves into schools. However, it was an academy called 'Attic Ten' that revolutionised the art of oratory and produced a famous student in Demosthenes, who is still considered the greatest orator of ancient Greece.

Following are the salient features of Demosthenes' oratory:

- He conceptualised oratory so that he could prosecute trustees of an inherited estate, who had cheated him.
- Patriotism was the basis of his speeches.
- He prepared his speeches perfectly before delivering them and
- his speeches were very clear, simple, concise and impressive.
- His oratory was vibrant yet very respectful.
- He believed focusing on a single subject and never losing sight of it.

The Orators of Rome

Ancient Rome produced some of the well-known orators of all times and the foremost among them is Marcus Cicero. He is believed to have designed the style and structure of modern oratory.

Cicero advocated the following features for a perfect speech:

- A good oration should not be restricted to one style.
- The speech should be prepared considering the requirements of the audience.
- The treatment of the subject should be flexible and varying. The speaker should attack, repeat, expand, expect protests, beseech and stress the important points.

- The vocabulary of the speech should be diverse and include synonyms, philosophical notes, verses and robust arguments.

Modern Trends of Oratory

18th Century: The 18th century oratory was marked by two extreme trends of oratory. Edmund Burke, one of the greatest orators of the 18th century, was known for delivering eloquent and purposeful speeches. On the other hand, Lord Chatham was an example of an orator, who believed in addressing a few elite class members. His speeches were of little purpose and stressed more on articulation than the subject (if there was one in them)

On the whole, the 18th century speeches constituted abundant allusions to Greek and Latin literature and was addressed primarily to the educated upper class.

19th Century: The 19th century was marked by a rise in religious speeches. This was due to the rise in preaching, primarily the Methodists and Puritans. Now, the speakers used biblical allusions rather than Greek allusions. Such speeches drew larger audiences than before. Actually, The end of the century saw audiences flocking in to listen to the more radical form of oratory.

20th Century: In the early years of the 20th century, oratory was marked by a radical style that was popularised by David Lloyd George. However, with time and advent of visual technology, oratory lost its appeal. The speeches were now delivered through a visual medium, i.e., television. Some people believe that dictators such as Adolf Hitler were responsible for the decline of oratory, as they inspired violence and negative patriotism through their speeches.

Development of Oratory in India

Unlike Greek or Roman civilizations, ancient India did not have a culture where oratory was used as a popular and effective tool to communicate with the public. While ancient India had a famous strategist like Chanakya and an emperor like Ashoka the Great, none could initiate or use oratory as well as the Greeks did. The only oratorical evidences of ancient India emerge from Indian mythology. Lord Krishna and Lord Rama were eloquent and articulate orators. In fact, Lord Krishna was the greatest orator in his own right. His speech to Arjuna on the verge of the War of Mahabharata has been turned into a holy book of the Hindus popularly known as 'Sri Bhagavad Gita'.

The author of the Mahabharata, Sri Ved Vyas is considered to be an excellent orator. He travelled to all parts of the country and attended many conferences to spread knowledge. He was a versatile scholar along with being a famous philosopher and poet.

Another scholar, who existed in India was Mahavira in 599 B.C. He was the exponent of Jainism and promoted non-violence, which he considered as the strongest weapon. Another great personality, who influenced people the world over was Lord Buddha. Lord Buddha renounced the world in order to solve the mystery behind life and death. Thereafter, he preached Buddhism and reformed the lives of many.

In the 8th century A.D., India was blessed with another philosopher and scholar Adi Shankaracharya. Shankaracharya created *maths* on the four corners of India and spread unity among the people of India. In the subsequent years, India experienced the presence of many scholars like Guru Nanak (the founder of Sikhism), Guru Ramdas, Dayanand Saraswati,

Ramkrishna Paramhansa, Swami Vivekananda and Yogiraj Arvind.

The mutiny of 1857 was a determined effort by India to gain independence. At this time, the people were rebelling against social, political and spiritual injustice. In response to the call of the times, a new kind of leadership arose. The whole country echoed with Bal Gangadhar Tilak' s call of 'freedom is our birthright'. This became the war cry of the freedom fighters. This simple statement personifies the style and simplicity of the great orators. They spoke to the people from the heart. They had a style, which was their own and signified the beginning of a new era in the writing of speeches.

Another speech, which has become immortal is Jawaharlal Nehru's speech at midnight on 15th August, 1947. The historic words 'At the stroke of midnight hour....' reverberate with the joy and jubilation of a leader, who spoke to the people of his aspirations and his hopes for the country. Dr. A.P.J. Kalam is another role model for the young aspiring orator.

However, the 20th century witnessed the greatest exponents of oratory in British India. Leaders such as Mahatma Gandhi, Subhash Chandra Bose and Lala Lajpat Rai instilled nationalism in millions of people through their dynamic speeches.

∞

Important Features of a Speech

The personality of orator: The public will listen to the orator, only if he is well known and charismatic. When Pt. Jawaharlal Nehru was the Prime Minster, the public thronged to listen to his speeches. Such was his charisma. Same can be said for many pre-independence orators such as Mahatma Gandhi, Lalaji and Tilak. The public always analyses the orator's standing in the society, his personality, his confidence and his opinion on important matters. Also, the orator needs to be distinguished by his way of dressing.

Topic: It is the topic of the speech that keeps the listeners hooked. Once the orator has identified the topic of the speech, he will have to complement it with appropriate elements such as emotions and voice modulation. The orator should choose the topic of the speech, which is interesting and relevant to the mood of the occasion and also not overlapping the time module.

Types of listeners: A successful orator always speaks on a topic with which listeners can associate themselves. It would be foolish for an orator to talk about pop music to a crowd of octogenarians, or talking about spirituality to a group of children.

Occasion: Last but not the least, a speaker should always feel the pulse of the occasion while delivering his speech.

∞

The Art of Speechmaking

In your life, you may have to face a situation where you will have to deliver a speech. Chances are that for the first time, you will be nervous and apprehensive even if you have rehearsed many times. Some people are natural orators, but even they have to work to master this art. While delivering a speech, you have to ensure that you do not bore your listeners. The speech should be interesting and must entail relevant contents to make an impact on the listeners. Has it ever happened that you were listening to a wonderful speaker and thought, "I wish I could speak like him." If someone else can speak in an impressive manner, so can you? Oratory is an art and it can be mastered with constant practice. Oratorical skills can be inborn or developed with time. You must have observed that there are always a few students, who are ready to speak on any topic. There are also some students, who are not able to speak even when they want to.

Nowadays, there are many institutes that offer courses to improve upon your communication skills. The print and electronic media is overflowing with the Ad culture, luring the public to gain fluency in a few weeks time. You can find plenty of such institutes in urban cities. There are many students and budding speakers, who are enrolling themselves to master the art. The Dale Carnegie Organisation in the US was the first to start such a course in the 1940s. The course became so popular and successful that now the organisation has its branches not only in the US, but all over the world.

In India also, such courses are coming up. The renowned speakers in India hail from politics, while in the west many heads of organisations such as 'Dell' and 'Microsoft' are as influential as their political counterparts. Our country boasts of orators, mostly in only two spheres: politics and religion. John Galbraith, who had served as a US ambassador to India, is famous for having said, "of all the races on earth, the Indians have the most nearly inexhaustible appetite for oratory." Pamila Philopose, columnist at the *Indian Express,* also claimed in one of her columns that the voice box of the Indians has neither the 'stop' button nor the 'volume' button.

Still, it is a fact that oratory is an art that can be mastered by persistent practice. The institutes make you speak in different and difficult situations to boost your confidence. Many famous personalities like Churchill, Kennedy and Bernard Shaw have accepted that they had to practise hard to become remarkable orators. When former England Prime Minister Disraeli made his first speech in the parliament, people present over there laughed at him. Disraeli shouted back at them, saying, "A day will come when you will hear me." He went to become one of England's foremost speakers.

Tips to become a Successful Orator

Identify the listeners: It is very important for the orator to identify his listeners. He has to see if they are literate or illiterate, rich or poor, young or old, etc. While campaigning for elections, an orator identifies the problems of the listeners and what is it that they want. It is also critical to get a solution to their problems. The text of a good speech touches the chord of the listener's heart.

Practice: Practice makes a man perfect and it stands true for the art of oratory as well. A gifted orator may not need to practise much, but many scholars have been seen getting nervous standing before a microphone! There are many ways to practise. If one is an amateur, he should not speak aloud or read the whole text. Instead, he should practise it by dividing it into parts. There is no need to memorise the script, but one should certainly work on his expressions. A charismatic orator always complements the right words with the right expressions.

Correct use of language: Oratory is nothing but speaking the right words at the right place. But one has to be careful here. Often, the speaker solemnly carries on with the speech and just concentrates on the plain facts. However, this can be very monotonous for the listeners and they might leave you speaking midway. To make your speech more interesting, infuse it with various emotions like anger, humour, passion and compassion that can inspire the listeners. A garnishing of emotion will make your speech more attractive and palatable.

Introducing yourself: Standing stiff like a statue in any gathering is not going to impress the crowd. The orator will have to present himself to the people, he is addressing. This does not mean that he will have to narrate his biography to them. All we suggest is that a good orator always lets listeners know about him like an open book.

Add correct dose of humour: If the speech's theme is not too serious, then the orator can add subtle humour to his speech. This will make the listeners laugh and remember his words for a long time. An orator does not need to practise this extensively. A humorous incident or a joke may add some spice to his otherwise solemn speech.

Present a solution, not a problem: If the orator talks about any kind of problem (water, electricity, etc.) in his speech, they should not be exaggerated or overdrawn. It is also necessary to offer possible solutions so that the listeners can relate it to themselves. You may talk about space technology with scientists, but to talk about it with rural dwellers will be foolishness and out of place. Moreover, they will not benefit anything from such talks.

Ways of Public Speaking

There are many ways of speaking in public. To speak in public, an orator can memorise the transcript, read it out, or can even deliver impromptu. This depends on many factors such as location, purpose and ambience of the speech.

Reading from a script: If the speaker has to speak in a seminar or formal get-together, then he can read from a script. This is because the script is usually empirical and lengthy.

Memorise the script or speak instinctively: A memorised speech will certainly be tailor-made, filled with appropriate words and facts. All that the orator has to do is to complement it with perfect presentation and remember the script of the speech. It is the latter that can be difficult to do. If the orator loses his memory midway, then all his efforts will be whitewashed. Therefore, seasoned orators speak instinctively to avoid an embarrassing situation.

Speaking instinctively: Many experienced orators till date have delivered speeches without preparing for them. They have judged the ambience of the location, the type of listeners and with their strong instincts, have delivered memorable and heartfelt speeches. One unforgettable example is of Dr. C.V. Raman, who had once started his speech by looking at a blade of grass in the precinct of his university. Rajneesh Osho used to begin his speeches by asking questions from the listeners – an interesting and effective way of speaking without memorising.

Impromptu speech: It can happen at times that one may be asked to speak unexpectedly at an occasion. It is difficult for one to refuse to speak, as he would be invited to speak because of his influential personality. If he is an experienced campaigner there will be no problem, but if the person is inexperienced then he may be left puzzled. The best thing in such a situation is to be relaxed and stress on one or two important points in the speech.

Categorisation of Speeches

The success of a speech lies in its motive. If the speaker is not aware of the motive of the speech (campaigning for election, collection of funds for charity, etc.) then his speech is nothing but a waste of time. Speeches can be categorised into infinite categories. Following are some of the common speech categories:

Religious Speeches: Earlier, religious speeches were confined to temples, gurudwaras, churches and mosques, but nowadays, there is no specified location for them. Religious speeches are inflammatory in nature and incite communal rites. Moreover, you can watch many television channels showing religious speeches by all and sundry. In foreign countries, there are various television channels for Presbyterian, Catholic, which show religious lectures throughout the day. Such channels are on a rise in India as well. Devotees from around the world, hear discourses by Sri Sai Baba on radio and television. In India, Adi Shankaracharya holds the primary place for such discourses. Following him closely are the lectures of Swami Dayanand Saraswati and Swami Vivekananda. Modern day art of living comes from leaders like Rajneesh Osho, Murari Bapu, Asaram Bapu and Sudhanshu Maharaj.

Constitutional Speeches (In judicial courts): Such speeches are delivered in courts to vindicate the accused or in defence of the accused. They are logical, empirical and evidence-based. Such elements make the speech more vigorous and convincing. In fact, the history of speechmaking began with court speeches. Court speeches were common in ancient Athens (Greece). In the 5th century BC (Golden Era of Athens), many renowned personalities made remarkable speeches in assemblies and courts. However, Cicero stands foremost amongst the ancient court orators. Cicero was also a writer, poet and politician, who lived in Rome. USA and England also have traditionally had court orators through ages. There were such orators from India as well such as Deshbandhu Chittaranjan Das, Motilal Nehru, Tej Bahadur Sapru, M.C.Setalvad and Nani Palkivala.

Political Speeches: In this category, orators can be divided into two subcategories. One, who deliver speeches in the parliament and second, who deliver speeches while campaigning for elections. Englishmen such as William Pit, John Wilkes, Edmund Burke, Macaulay, Disraeli, Gladstone and Winston Churchill were exceptional political orators. Political orators in India emerged with the independence movement. Pre-eminent political orators in India have been Madan Mohan Malviya, Dadabhai Naoroji, Gokhale, Lal-Bal-Pal, Arvind Ghosh, Jawaharlal Nehru, Ram Manohar Lohia, Jaiprakash Narayan and many others. The famous personalities, who made astounding Parliamentary speeches include Prakash Vir Shastri, Piloo Modi, Krishna Menon, Feroz Gandhi among many others. Atal Bihari Vajpayee is considered to be a vigorous orator from the opposition. Modern day parliamentarians like Sushma Swaraj, Arun Jaitley and Jyotiraditya Scindia have also nurtured into impressive orators.

One name that differs from all these is that of Krishna Menon, who made the lengthiest speech in the United

Nations on the Kashmir issue. However, the man who really stands out among all is Mahatma Gandhi. Gandhi's speeches began in South Africa where he fought against apartheid (racial discrimination). He also delivered unforgettable speeches against the British in India. He epitomised the art of oratory better than anyone else. His speeches comprised all the necessary elements of effective oratory.

Literary Speeches: Literary and figurative lectures and speeches are usually delivered at book launches, seminars, etc. George Bernard Shaw and William Lyon Phelps have been the pioneers when it comes to such speeches. Some of the Indian personalities famous for their literary speeches are Mahadevi Verma, Narendra Sharma, Prabhakar Machve, Harivansh Rai Bachchan, Namvar Singh, Rajendra Yadav and Ashok Vajpayee. Here it would also be appropriate to mention about Prabhash Joshi, an eminent journalist who has the gift of writing and speaking immaculately.

Public Speeches: Under this category, those speakers are included who are obliged to deliver speeches once in a while because of their position. They may speak on certain incidents and occasions. In this category, we may include bureaucrats from the domain of the Civil Service.

Academic Speeches & Scientific Speeches: Such speeches are usually delivered by academicians, scientists, literati and educationists. This category includes personalities like Dr. Radhakrishnan, Dr. Rajendra Prasad and Dr. Zakir Hussain. They were remarkable politicians and most learned men of India. Similarly, Sir J.C. Bose, Sir C.V. Raman and Dr. A.P.J. Abdul Kalam lectured on the inaugurations of the All India Science Congress.

∞

Classification of Speeches

1. **Informative Speeches:** Such speeches are often called lectures as they are delivered in university, school classrooms and conferences. Such lectures discuss a particular topic or subject in detail.

2. **Occasional Speeches:** Such speeches are delivered on special occasions such as inauguration or felicitation. Normally, the speaker praises or felicitates a person through such speeches and hails the harbinger of an oncoming event.

3. **Entertaining Speeches:** Such speeches are hilarious and are solely meant to entertain the audience in a lighter vein.

OO

Arranging the Order of a Speech

A good speaker always knows what will keep his listeners interested in the speech. He not only speaks what listeners want to listen, but also cleverly incorporates his thoughts in between the speech. To become an effective speaker, however, one should speak his thoughts or objectives in a proper order. A speaker can very well write it on a paper and then speak out.

While preparing for a speech, a speaker should follow the following order:

- Bring together all the thoughts and the messages that he wants to convey to the listeners.
- Then arrange them in an appropriate order.
- Read again and again the order of the ingredients of the speech.
- While reading, incorporate the points that have been left out.
- Finally, read out the speech confidently with a positive body language.

The presentation of the speech should be natural. A good speaker always breaks his schedule time into small sessions while delivering a speech. Ideally, the speech time should be divided into three sessions. For the first 20 per cent of the time, the speaker should make it clear to the listeners, what he actually wants to convey through the speech. The next 70 percent of the time should be devoted discussing about the core issues supported by appropriate examples. In the last ten percent of the time, the speaker should sum-up the main points of the speech.

Remember, both the beginning and the ending of a speech are crucial and should be said very carefully. In the beginning, the speaker has to involve the audience in the speech. The beginning should be simple, terse and articulate. In the beginning, one can narrate a story or co-relate an interesting example. One should never begin his speech with a negative note.

Similarly, the ending of the speech should be as interesting and intriguing. The speaker should not divert from the main topic, when ending the speech and the ending should leave an everlasting effect on the audience.

Presentation

Presentation is a vital aspect while delivering a speech. A good speaker uses a variety of ways to get his point across to the listeners. Presentation of a speech includes various factors such as body language, voice modulation and pace of speech.

To make a perfect presentation, a speaker should begin his speech at a slow but fluent pace. He should be aware of the time limitation in his mind. Gradually, he can increase the pace of the speech but should not let it become so fast that it loses its effect. While speaking, the speaker should involve the audience. If the day of speech is of any significance, then the speaker should certainly mention it somewhere in his speech. The last line ideally should be the conclusion of the whole speech. If the speech is delivered to promote a product, say a book, or in an interactive programme, then it can be concluded with a question-answer round.

OO

Body Language

The body language of a speaker plays a very important and vital role while delivering a speech. The look of the speaker, his eyes and the way he moves – all reflect his confidence. All great orators of all times have had a very positive and impressive body language. They have looked confident even when they had to deliver an impromptu speech. Some of the great orators had a certain style of speaking, which could only be associated with them. No one can forget the 'V' sign immortalised by Winston Churchill during World War. The 'V' sign symbolised the victory achieved by the English forces and soon everyone in the world was using it. Even now, many leaders and sportspersons use the 'V' sign by raising their two fingers to signify victory.

To make the speech more effective, the speaker should make appropriate gestures, mould the facial expressions and add a spark in his eyes. A person might be a specialist in his field but it is not necessary that he will be a good speaker also. To be a good speaker, he will have to practise hard. It is important to remain calm before and during the speech, as the signs of nervousness may be reflected through the body language. Signs of nervousness include frequent biting of nails, scratching of head, closing and opening of shirt buttons, readjusting the knot of necktie, etc.

A speaker should look out for following factors concerning his body language:

The standing posture: The way a speaker stands reflects a lot about his attitude. If he stands leisurely, it seems that he has a casual approach to the speech. On the other hand, if he stands in attention, he might look slightly funny and also very formal and authoritative. A speaker should be relaxed while speaking and stand straight. His body should not bend on any of the sides. A smile on the face and a confident look along with a good posture will always impress the listeners.

Focus the look at the audience: While delivering a speech, it is imperative for the speaker to look towards the audience. If the speaker looks towards the ceiling while speaking then his audience will not feel involved and will feel alienated. It is not possible to look at each member of the audience (assuming it is a large audience), but the speaker should always look in the direction of the audience. This will make the audience feel that the speaker is directly talking to them. Remember how newsreaders on television look at the camera, as if they were talking to you.

OO

Introduction

Global leaders for ages have used speeches as their most effective tool to influence masses. From India, great orators like Gandhi, Nehru, Bose, Tilak, Lala Lajpat Rai have delivered historically significant speeches that made millions of people follow them. Their words, supported by high vigour and commitment, played a pivotal role in the outgoing of the British government from India. Gandhi, especially, was a major crowd puller when he delivered his speeches. He was the mass leader and gave direction to the suppressed Indians. When the British attacked the Indian freedom fighters, he gave them a unique tool to fight – that of non-violence. Never before in history had such a tool rested in any of the fighter's armour. Many laughed at this but the loin-clothed man had faith in his decision. His determination combined appropriately with his inspirational addresses to the nation, which when gathered momentum, weighed heavily on the British. Such was the power of his words. Gandhi's rhetoric speeches were well supported in pre-independence India by natural orators like Nehru, Tilak, Bose and Lalaji. Nehru, a dynamic speaker on the stage, has addressed the nation more than any other Indian leader till date. His enthusiasm, sophistication and ability to pace his speech made him a truly wonderful orator. His speech on the Independence eve of India still echoes aloud, best summarising the sacrifices made by our freedom fighters.

On the other hand, extremists like Bose gave oratory a new definition. Bose stimulated his army of soldiers by using loud and dynamic phrases like 'Give me blood and I shall give you freedom'. Who can forget the immortal speech of Tilak when he said 'Swaraj is my birthright and I shall have it'. Similarly, there were magnetic speeches of Lalaji and Madame Bhikaji Cama that internationalised the Indian cause of independence. After the demise of Nehru, India has unfortunately missed leaders with influential oratorical skills, especially in modern India.

It is impossible to ignore the terrific speeches that were delivered in the western world. Rousing speakers like Roosevelt, Kennedy, Dr. Martin Luther King, Churchill, Lincoln and Stalin made significant changes in the course of history with their speeches. Their speeches deeply influenced the people of their nations. Their talks were walked by millions of people, and this effect of theirs made them statesmen of supreme stature. Theodore Roosevelt mobilised the whole of US when he urged people to get rid of a life of sloth and embrace strenuous life; flamboyant President John F. Kennedy urged the people to 'Ask not what the country can do for you, ask what you can do for the country'and Dr. Martin Luther King spoke openly of a dream of America with a sense of oneness. Abraham Lincoln revitalised the war-affected America by a small speech with a never-ending influence.

During the World War, Churchill and Stalin rose to the occasion to bring the nation together against the powerful army of Adolf Hitler. Churchill, who was sworn in as the prime minister of England during the World War, said before the parliament, "I have nothing to offer but blood, toil, tears and sweat." His words motivated his soldiers enough and they countered the enemy army with utmost courage and vigour. Another speech that made a major influence during the war was that of Joseph Stalin, who asked his countrymen to "fight till the last drop of our blood."

It is true to say that words that are spoken by truly great people hold greater meaning. One such great personality whose words have also influenced leaders across the globe is Nelson Mandela – In his youth, a pillar of determination and in his current years, an epitome of solemn speeches that are considered no less than holy sermons. His addresses to the public against the tyranny of white government united the citizenry of South Africa and it was in 1993 that he realised his dream.

In the ancient years, it was the philosophical 'Apology' of Socrates that is even adored in the modern world. Perhaps, too modern for his times, Socrates was a man beyond the understanding of early Athenians, who sentenced him to death. Socrates' address to his fellow citizens familiarises us with the subtle usage of words and his rich knowledge of philosophy and metaphysics that was unheard of till those times.

Speeches have been used for various motives – peace, war, atrocity, compassion, inspiration, or maybe humour. It is hard to present a collection of all speeches in one book, as each has its own relevance. However, we have, in this book, speeches that are intriguing as well as inspirational. We have precisely included the speeches from all aspects of life that will touch the heart of young Indians and spread invaluable messages of all-time greats amongst them. It can be an incredibly enriching experience to study these speeches, which were designed many a times before being delivered.

∞

Preparation of a Speech

It is necessary to prepare for a speech before you step on the stage. Without adequate preparation, a speaker can often get nervous while speaking and forget the right words. Such a situation can certainly be very embarrassing for any speaker. If he is a renowned speaker or a politician, it can be very insulting too. The bigger the speaker is in stature, the better should be his preparation. Preparing for a speech is not easy. One has to practise for long hours to deliver a perfect speech and if someone is a beginner then he may have to practise even harder.

Pre-independence
Speeches from India

Mahatma Gandhi

Father of the Nation

Born: 2nd October, 1869
Died: 30th January, 1948

"Generations to come will scarce believe that such a one as this walked the earth in flesh and blood." These words were said by Albert Einstein, the world's greatest scientist and noble laureate, for Mahatma Gandhi. Born in 1869 at Porbandar, Mahatma Gandhi constantly fought against the British forces to attain freedom for India.

Mahatma Gandhi, known as India's 'Father of the Nation', was a qualified lawyer from Great Britain. After becoming a lawyer, he went to Durban, South Africa to practise law. It was there that he was ill-treated by the British, who controlled South Africa that time. He was so deeply touched by the plight of the blacks that he decided to devote his life to fight against racial discrimination and imperialism. He returned to India and protested against the British government. However, he used a unique weapon to fight against the British Raj – Non-violence. Gandhi is still known worldwide for his doctrine of non-violence.

Gandhi led many movements against the British, including Salt March, Civil Disobedience Movement and Quit India Movement. In 1920, Gandhi adopted the Non-violence Non-cooperation movement against the unjust British, and hundreds of thousands of people thronged after him echoing his thoughts. He also wrote three articles for 'Young India' urging people to join the movement. The British took it as an opportunity to arrest Gandhi, accusing him of provoking violence. His trial was followed at Ahmedabad on March 23, 1922, where he pleaded guilty and delivered a speech that best reflected the views of the great man. Gandhi was sentenced to six years' imprisonment after this speech.

Non-violence is the First Article of My Faith

Non-violence is the first article of my faith. It is the last article of my faith. I am here not to submit to a light penalty but to the highest penalty. I do not ask for mercy. I am here, therefore, to invite and submit to the highest penalty that can be inflicted upon me for what in law is a deliberate crime and what appears to me to be the highest duty of a citizen. Mr. Judge, by the time I have finished with my statement you will, perhaps have a glimpse of what is raging within my breast to run this maddest risk which a sane man can run.

This is what Gandhi read out before the court:

My public life began in 1893 in South Africa in troubled weather. My first contact with the British authority in that country was not of a happy character. I discovered that as a man and an Indian, I had no rights. On the contrary, I discovered that I had no rights as a man because I was an Indian.

But I was not baffled. I thought that this treatment of Indians was an excrescence upon a system that was intrinsically and mainly good. I gave the government my voluntary and hearty cooperation, criticising it fully where I felt it was faulty but never wishing its destruction.

In South Africa, in 1899, when the existence of the Empire was threatened, I offered my services to it, raised a volunteer ambulance corps and served at several actions that took place for the relief. Similarly, in 1906, at the time of the Zulu revolt, I raised a stretcher-bearer party and served till the end of the 'rebellion'. On both these occasions, I received medals and was even mentioned in dispatches. For my work in South Africa, I was given a Kaiser-I-Hind Gold Medal. When the war broke out in 1914 between England and Germany, I raised a volunteer ambulance corps in London consisting of the then resident Indians in London, chiefly students. Its work was acknowledged by the authorities to be valuable. In all these efforts at service, I was actuated by the belief that it was possible by such services to gain a status of full equality in the Empire for my new countrymen.

The first shock came in the shape of the Rowlatt Act, a law designed to rob people of all real freedom. I felt called upon to lead an intensive agitation against it. Then followed the Punjab horrors beginning with the massacre at Jallianwala Bagh to public floggings and other indescribable humiliations. The Punjab crime was whitewashed and most culprits went not only unpunished but remained in service and some continued to draw pensions from the Indian revenue, and in some cases were been rewarded. I saw too that not only did the reforms not mark a change of heart, but they were only a method of further draining India off her wealth.

I came reluctantly to the conclusion that the British connection had made India more helpless that she ever was before, politically and economically. She has become so poor that she has little power of resisting famines. The cottage industry, so vital for India's existence, has been ruined by incredibly heartless and inhuman processes as described by English witnesses.

Little do town-dwellers know how the semi-starved masses of Indians are slowly sinking to lifelessness. Little do they know that their miserable comfort represents the brokerage they get for the work they do for foreign exploiter, that the profits and the brokerage are sucked from the masses.

My experience of political cases in India leads me to the conclusion that in nine out of every ten, the condemned men were totally innocent. Their crime consisted in love of their country. In ninety-nine cases out of a hundred, justice has been denied to Indians as against Europeans in the courts of India. This is not an exaggerated picture. It is the experience of almost every Indian, who has had anything to do with such cases.

Section 124-A under which I am happily charged is perhaps the prince among the political sections of the Indian Penal Code designed to suppress the liberty of the citizen. Affection cannot be regulated by law. Of one has no affection for a person or thing, one should be free to give the fullest expression to his disaffection so long as he does not contemplate, promote, or incite to violence. But the section under which I am charged is the one under which mere promotion of disaffection is crime. I have studied some of the cases tried under it, and I know that some of the most loved of India's patriots have been convicted under it. I consider it a privilege, therefore, to be charged under it. I have endeavoured to give in the briefest outline of the reasons for my disaffection. I have no personal ill-will against single administrator. But I hold it to be a virtue to be disaffected towards a government which in its totality has done harm to India than any previous system. India is less manly under the British rule than she ever was before. Holding such a belief, I consider it to be a sin to have affection for the system. And it has been a precious privilege for me to be able to write what I have in various articles tendered in evidence against me.

In fact, I believe that I have rendered a service to India and England by showing in Non-cooperation, the way out of the unnatural state in which both are living. In my humble opinion, non-cooperation with the evil is as much a duty as is cooperation with the good.

I am here to invite and submit cheerfully to the highest penalty that can be inflicted upon me for what in law is deliberate crime and what happens to me be the highest duty of a citizen. The only course open to you, Mr. Judge, is either to resign your post and thus dissociate yourself from evil if you feel that the law called upon to administer is an evil and that in reality, I am innocent, or to inflict on me the severest penalty if you believe that the system and the law you are assisting to administer are good for the people of this country and that activity is therefore injurious to the public weal.

Lala Lajpat Rai

Punjab Kesari

Born: 28th January, 1865
Died: 17th November, 1928

When the British ruled our motherland, there was one fighter, who fought bravely against the British and even sacrificed his life in the process. He was Lala Lajpat Rai, also called Lalaji. Born on January 28, 1865, he was called the 'Lion of Punjab' because of his brave deeds against the British. In those days, when India was under the clouds of colonization, he spread India's cause for freedom all over the world. He formed Indian Home Rule League of New York in 1917 to spread awareness about the atrocities of the British in India. His fearless and passionate life ended a few days after he was hit on the chest in a lathi-charge by the British policemen.

In 1928, the British government formed a group of parliamentarians called Simon Commission headed by John Simon. It was given the powers to control the acts and reformations of India, but it did not even include one Indian. The Simon Commission was therefore, condemned by every Indian, and Lalaji was one of the major leaders, who led demonstrations against the Simon Commission. He delivered a speech on February 16, 1928 in the Legislative Council to speak of his views and the views of the fellow demonstrators. The speech was highly dynamic and well applauded by the leaders nationally.

Boycott Simon Commission

Before I begin I would like to very categorically and concisely give you the reasons for the action I take up. First of all, I do not trust the bonafide of the people or government, who have set up this commission. Secondly, I do not have a high opinion of the abilities of the people, who comprise the commission. I admit that Sir John Simon, who is one of the members is very able and has the best of intentions and motives but on the whole, they are ignorant of India, its history and its politics. Without this knowledge, I think they will not be qualified enough to carry out the task, they are entrusted with. The commission has been given too short a time to fulfil their tasks. The gods themselves wouldn't have been able to complete this task in this short time – the task is so complicated. They cannot make any recommendations, which are wise enough to be acceptable to both India and England. The members of the commission are so scared that they cannot go out and communicate with the people and inform them of their program. They are very secretive about their movements and nobody knows where and how they move/travel.

Thirdly, I do not trust that this commission will be able to solve the problems that face our country today. India's problems are such that a commission cannot solve them. It needs representatives from both India and England to sit together and work out a solution.

The Secretary of the State speaks of the glorious association of India and England. According to him, the British saved India from anarchy and if the Britishers leave India then India will again be thrown into the arms of anarchy. He asserts that the Parliament has done a favour to India by taking away the government from the hands of the East India Company. The Britishers view is different from mine. They might think that their association with India is glorious and beneficial for India but I think it is shameful and harmful. I cannot think of any way in which this association has been beneficial to India. My viewpoint and that of the Secretary of the State is very different.

He thinks that India has been saved from anarchy. What does he know of anarchy? The greatest anarchy is to live under the yoke of a foreign power, to be ruled by a government, which does not allow you to have a say in making the laws that shape your destiny.

If we bow down before these unnecessary fears of Anarchy, we can never progress. I am not afraid from this House I can say that. I am ready to face any anarchy, which might prevail, once the Britishers leave. If we have faced them, we can face anything. There cannot be anything worse than this. What can be lower than this slavery? If the British think that we will fight & fall apart- I am ready to face that also. We have been fighting with each other for so many years. Now it is time to settle our differences and form some kind of government. I can see that some members of the European Community are laughing at me. I say 'Laugh' you can afford to laugh. You are like the painter, who cannot paint his own picture clearly. If you had to bear what we have to, you too would not be laughing. If we had ruled England even for a span of two years, you would be weeping not laughing.

Towards Freedom

This speech was delivered by Lalaji in Mumbai on February 20, 1920, when he had returned to India after advocating India's cause across the western world.

This is neither the time nor the occasion to express my opinion on the political condition of the country. I will however present my thoughts and views on the 'young India' today. It gives me great pleasure to announce that from now the fundamental principle of Hindu-Muslim unity will be a great asset to the political future of the country. This shall not be a short-term goal but a long abiding truth which we will stand by all our lives and till we attain freedom. Even after that we will live like brothers, who are set to win. This is the basic principle, which we need to adopt as the first article of our political belief.

The second principle is that we must have complete faith in ourselves. We can be successful only if we believe in our efforts. "Nations are made by themselves". We can take guidance, cooperation and advice in certain matters but not patronage and dictation in all matters. We are not children but a mature nation with the wisdom of 6000 years behind us.

In my travels across the world, I have come across three great independent and self-governing nations i.e. the Japanese, American and the English. I realised that we equal them in all areas except maybe modern technology. We have been inferior in not being able to unite, in adapting to the modern times to a certain extent and also may be in learning the lessons of modern diplomacy. We too might have been considered a great 'self-governing nation' if we had learnt to sweep away our past and entered the field of violence and had learnt to tell lies on a grandiose scale. We might lack these so called qualities but I would like you to learn one quality. We have always stood for the righteous and tried to win on the basis of righteousness. In this way, you should try to be honest to your nation. Seek the truth, speak the truth and act the truth. If you do that I promise you that victory shall be yours. People are fighting for superiority. We, however, only want to be considered equal.

People might be tempted by the call of imperialism and even want to be partners in the great imperial game. I have however never felt the desire to be a part of this system. I feel that there is no word coined by man more vicious, criminal and sinful than 'imperialism'.

OO

Jawaharlal Nehru

The First Prime Minister of India

Born: 14th November, 1889
Died: 27th May, 1964

Born on November 14, 1889 in Allahabad, Pandit Jawaharlal Nehru was the first prime minister of independent India. He was also a famous freedom fighter, and worked with Gandhiji in the Indian National Congress. He was imprisoned several times by the British. As Prime Minister (1947-64) of free India, he developed the economy and the status of independent India. He died on May 27, 1964. 'Fondly called Chacha Nehru' by children because of his love for children, his birthday is celebrated as Children's Day in India.

Nehru was an orator of highest quality. His dynamic speeches still inspire the leaders of modern India. Two of his speeches given below, are acclaimed masterpieces. 'Tryst with Destiny' was delivered by Nehru on the eve of India's independence (August 15, 1947) from the British. 'The light has gone out' was an emotional address to the nation on the January 30, 1948 when his mentor and Father of the Nation, Gandhi was assassinated.

Tryst with Destiny

Long years ago, we made a tryst with destiny, and now the time comes when we shall redeem our pledge, not wholly or in full measure, but very substantially. At the stroke of the midnight hour, when the world sleeps, India will awake to life and freedom. A moment comes, which comes but rarely in history, when we step out from the old to the new, when an age ends, and when the soul of a nation, long suppressed, finds utterance. It is fitting that at this solemn moment, we take the pledge of dedication to the service of India and her people and to the still larger cause of humanity.

At the dawn of history, India started on her unending quest, and trackless centuries are filled with her striving and the grandeur of her success and her failures. Through good and ill fortune alike, she has never lost sight of that quest or forgotten the ideals which gave her strength. We end today a period of ill fortune and India discovers herself again. The achievement we celebrate today is but a step, an opening of opportunity, to the greater triumphs and achievements that await us. Are we brave enough and wise enough to grasp this opportunity and accept the challenge of the future?

Freedom and power bring responsibility. The responsibility rests upon this Assembly, a sovereign body representing the sovereign people of India. Before the birth of freedom, we have endured all the pains of labour and our hearts are heavy with the memory of this sorrow. Some of those pains continue even now. Nevertheless, the past is over and it is future that beckons to us now.

That future is not one of ease or resting but of incessant striving so that we may fulfil the pledges, we have so often taken and the one we shall take today. The service of India means the service of the millions, who suffer. It means the ending of poverty and ignorance and disease and inequality of opportunity. The ambition of the greatest man of our generation has been to wipe every tear from every eye. That may be beyond us, but as long as there are tears and suffering, so long our work will not be over.

And so we have to labour and to work, and work hard, to give reality to our dreams. Those dreams are for India, but they are also for the world, for all the nations and peoples are too closely knit together today for anyone of them to imagine that it can live apart. Peace has been said to be indivisible; so is freedom, so is prosperity now, and so also is disaster in this One World that can no longer be split into isolated fragments.

To the people of India, whose representatives we are, we make an appeal to join us with faith and confidence in this great adventure. This is no time for petty and destructive criticism, no time for ill-will or blaming others. We have to build the noble mansion of free India where all her children may dwell.

The Light has Gone Out

Friends and comrades, the light has gone out of our lives and there is darkness everywhere. I do not know what to tell you and how to say it. Our beloved leader, Bapu as we called him, the Father of the Nation, is no more. Perhaps, I am wrong to say that. Nevertheless, we will not see him again as we have seen him for these many years. We will not run to him for advice and seek solace from him, and that is a terrible blow, not to me only but to millions and millions in this country. And it is a little difficult to soften the blow by any other advice that I or anyone else can give you.

The light has gone out, I said, and yet I was wrong. For the light that shone in this country was no ordinary light. The light that has illumined this country for these many years will illumine this country for many more years later, that light will still be seen in this country and the world will see it and it will give solace to innumerable hearts. For that light represented something more than the immediate present; it represented the living, the eternal truths, reminding us of the right path, drawing us from error, taking this ancient country to freedom.

All this has happened when there was so much more for him to do. We could never think that he was unnecessary or that he had done his task. But now, particularly, when we are faced with so many difficulties, his not being with us is a blow most terrible to bear.

A mad man has put an end to his life, for I can only call him mad, who did it and yet there has been enough of poison spread in this country during the past years and months, and this poison has had an effect on people's minds. We must face this poison, we must root out this poison, and we must face all the perils that encompass us, and face them not madly or badly, but rather in the way that our beloved teacher taught us to face them.

We have to behave like strong and determined people, determined to face all the perils that surround us, determined to carry out the mandate that our great teacher and our great leader has given us, remembering always that if, as I believe, his spirit looks upon us and sees us, nothing would displease his soul so much as to see that we have indulged in any small behaviour or any violence.

So we must not do that. But that does not mean that we should be weak, but rather that we should, in strength and in unity, face all the troubles that are in front of us. We must hold together, and all our petty troubles and difficulties and conflicts must be ended in the face of this great disaster. A great disaster is a symbol to us to remember all the big, things of life and forget the small things of which we have thought too much. In his death, he has reminded us of the big things of life, the living truth, and if we remember that, then it will be well with India.

And while we pray, the greatest prayer that we can offer is to take a pledge to dedicate ourselves to the truth, and to the cause for which this great countryman of ours lived and for which he has died. That is the best prayer that we can offer him and his memory. That is the best prayer that we can offer to India and ourselves.

OO

Bal Gangadhar Tilak

The Lion of India

Born: 2nd July, 1856
Died: 1st August, 1920

Born in 1856, Bal Gangadhar Tilak is remembered for his immortal and inspiring words: "Freedom is my birthright and I shall have it."

Tilak was a passionate freedom fighter and writer. He was the founder of newspaper 'Kesri' which exists even today. He emphasised widely on 'swaraj' (self-rule) and wrote many articles urging people to fight for it. In 1908, the British jailed him in Burma accusing him of provoking people. When, in 1914, he returned to India, he received a hero's welcome. He had a massive following and this was witnessed when over 20, 00,000 people gathered at Mumbai beach to mourn his death.

He remained a hero forever, and a mentor to many, including Mahatma Gandhi. He delivered an astounding speech on May 17, 1917 in which he laid stress on 'swaraj'. Each word of this speech inspired the young and old of the nation. Given below is the transcript of the famous speech.

Freedom is my Birthright

I might be physically old but my spirit is young. I want to be eternally youthful. What I will speak today will remain young forever. Just as the body becomes old but the spirit remains young, in the same way, there might seem to be slowing down of the independence movement but the desire, the spirit is alive and eternal. It will not rest till we are liberated. Freedom is our birthright and we shall have it. As long as this spirit is alive within me, I cannot be old. It is eternal. The winds cannot wither it, weapons cannot cut it, and fire cannot destroy it. If we ask for self-government, we shall get it. We all have this spirit of liberty within us. We just need to awaken it. I want to remove the bondage of ignorant and selfish minds.

We all know what self-government means! Don't we all want it? Would you tolerate a stranger coming into your house and ruling over your kitchen? We all have the right to govern ourselves as we wish. People tell us we are not fit for self-government. I ask if the British have not made us able enough to rule ourselves, is it not time, we rose and made ourselves fit enough for self government?

If we want to be fit, we have to fight for it and for this, we need an efficient organisation. Our Congress has become too slow and archaic for this task. It moves slowly and cannot face the challenges. Mere demonstrations are not enough. Now we need determined and firm action, which can be enforced by the most disciplined members in the organisation. We must not only pass a resolution but also act on it. 'Discipline' is the key to success for the Congress. Uncontrolled crowds and mobs cannot achieve anything. We will have to sacrifice individual self for the welfare of the country.

The spirit of the nation has to be saved. This is our main duty. Our country can benefit only if we preserve 'swaraj'. The Congress has already passed a law of self-government. There are various objections to this from vested politicians. The main objection is the illiteracy of the majority of the nation. I feel that if the literate have even a vague idea of 'swaraj' that should be enough. The illiterates do manage their own affairs. Illiteracy does not make one an idiot. If they can manage their lives, they can manage 'swaraj' also. The illiterate too have the right to live their lives. We need to awaken the spirit within them. It is not only the need but our duty also. They too have the right to dream and live a full life. The call has already gone out. "Now or Never". Rectitude and a Constitutional struggle is only required. Move forward and have trust in God. His compassion shall frame the final issue.

Subhash Chandra Bose

The Fiery Revolutionary

Born: 23rd January, 1897
Died: 18th August, 1945

Subhash Chandra Bose was an Indian freedom fighter, who had built a huge army of freedom fighters called the Indian National Army to free India from the British Raj. Born on January 23, 1897, Bose was imprisoned and beaten many times by the British during his struggle for freedom but his passion to free India was so strong that he fought continuously. He finally died from burns suffered in a plane crash.

Bose was also a terrific orator and this can be largely proved by the high voltage speeches he delivered to his army. Amongst his many speeches, two speeches, 'To Delhi! To Delhi' and 'Give me blood, and I promise you freedom' remain immortal. In the former, Bose urges his soldiers and officers to be tough and fight till the freedom is achieved, while in the latter speech, Bose urges his young soldiers and officers to fight incessantly against the British tyranny.

To Delhi! To Delhi!

Speech at a military review of the Indian National Army, July 5, 1943.

Soldiers of India's Army of Liberation!

I am very proud of being here with you today. Providence has given me the honour of announcing to the world that the Indian Liberation Army has come to its own. Today it has been drawn up in the military formation on the front in Singapore.

This army will not just help India attain freedom from the British yoke, but will also form the national army of free India. Every Indian should be proud of the fact that an army by Indians has been organised under their own leader. It will be a historic moment when it goes to battle.

There was a time when it was thought that India – the land over which the sun does not set – was immortal. I have never thought this way. I have learnt from history that every empire has its decline and collapse. I have also seen how cities, which once formed the bulwarks of the nation, have now been reduced to mere graveyards. Today, when we stand on the graveyard of the British Raj, even a child is convinced that the British empire is something of the past.

In 1939, when France declared war on Germany, there was but one cry on everyone's lips: "To Paris, To Paris!" In 1941, when the brave soldiers of Japan set out on their historic march, the cry was: "To Singapore, To Singapore!"

Comrades! Soldiers! Your battle cry has to be: "To Delhi, To Delhi!" I do not know how many of us will survive this war of independence but I do know that we will finally be victorious. We shall not rest till we celebrate victory on another graveyard of the British Raj – the Red Fort of Old Delhi.

All through my public career, I have thought that India is matured for independence, but what it did not have was only one thing, an army of liberation. Each one of you should be proud of the honour and privilege bestowed on you by being a part of the Indian National Army. You have been the first ones to come and organise the army. You have to be proud of being the vanguards of a noble cause like this.

I should also tell you once again that you have two-fold task in your hands. The independence will have to be won with the force of arms and cost of blood. When our motherland attains freedom, you will have to be the permanent force of the country and protect the freedom. We have to make our nation such a strong force that never again will it become slave to any foreign power.

You are the soldiers and you will have to enjoy and follow three ideals of fidelity, duty and sacrifice. Those soldiers, who remain loyal to their country and ready to sacrifice their lives for the motherland can never die; they become unconquerable. By embracing these three ideals, you will also become unconquerable. Engrave these three ideals in your heart.

Military and spiritual training are prerequisites for soldiers. Everyone of you should train yourself and your comrades in such a way that you have ultimate confidence in your abilities, be unafraid of death and have the courage to take initiative in a precarious situation if at all it arises. You have witnessed the excellent results that the merging of scientific results and bravery, courage and dynamism can achieve. Take a lesson from all this and construct a first-rate army for Mother India.

I would like to say to the officers amongst you that your responsibility is very heavy. Your responsibility is far greater than the responsibility of the officers of the rest of the armies of the world. We have to forget what the British taught us and learn what they did not teach us. Yet, I am confident that you will be able to carry out the task that our countrymen have thrown on you, courageous soldiers. Always remember that officers can make or spoil an army. Also do not forget that the reason for the defeats of the British at many fronts has been their incompetent officers. Also remember that the army of free India will be born out of you.

I would also like to tell everyone of you that during this war, you will have to gain the experience and attain the success which can solely build the national tradition of the future army. An army without courage, bravery and invincibility cannot fight against a powerful enemy.

Comrades! You have accepted the mission that is truly the greatest a man can work for. To complete this mission, no sacrifice will be great, not even if you sacrifice your life. Today you stand as the guardians of the country's national honour and embodiment of country's ambitions and expectations. Therefore, behave in such a way that the Indians bless you and the generations to come be proud of you.

I have stated that today is the proudest day of my life. For men of British India, there cannot be a better honour, better pride than being the first soldier in the army of liberation. However, this honour also has responsibility attached with it and I am wholly aware of it. I commit you that I will be with you in all the times – sunshine and darkness, joy and sorrow, defeat and victory. Who among us will live to see a free India does not affect us. What is important is that India will become free and we will give our best to make it free. May the Providence bless us and help achieve freedom for our army.

Inqualab Zindabad! Azad Hind Zindabad!

Give me Blood, and I Promise you Freedom!

(Speech at a rally of Indians in Burma, July 4, 1944)

Friends!

In East Asia, twelve months ago, a new programme of 'total mobilisation' or 'maximum sacrifice' was placed before the Indians. I shall briefly recount on accomplishments of the past year, and also put before you our demands for the coming year. Before I move forward, I would also impress upon you the importance of this marvellous opportunity of attaining freedom from the British. The British are fighting on many fronts, and losing in most of them. Our chances of attaining freedom have rapidly increased because the British have abated because of the wearing war. Thus, our task has become easier than it was five years back. Such a golden opportunity to get rid of the enemy cannot be missed. Let us swear to fully utilise this opportunity to set our country free from the British yoke.

My optimism is not just based on the fact that three million Indians in East India support the cause. It is also supported by the fact that a huge movement is going on inside India and millions of Indians are ready to undergo any suffering to liberate the country.

It is unfortunate that since the war of 1857, our countrymen have been deprived of all arms, while the enemy has all the weapons and armoury at its disposal. In this age, it is not possible to win the battle without arms and weapons. By God's grace, Indians in East Asia have managed to procure weapons for a modern army. Also, in East Asia, there are no communal differences that the British can use to mar our chances of movement. Now, we have an ideal combination of circumstances that favour the success of this venture. Now, Indians will have to come forward themselves to pay the price of liberty. 'Total mobilisation' requires men, money and materials. As far as men are concerned, enough recruitments have been done till now.

The problem of supplies and transport has to be solved, mobilisation of men, money and material has to be continued.

Volunteers at Home Front should never forget that East Asia, especially Burma, is the base for the war of liberation. It is not a war between armies but a 'Total war'. Therefore, we cannot afford to have a weak base.

Friends, a year back, I had pledged to give you a second front if you gave me 'total mobilisation'. I will take a step further now. The first stage of the war has finished. Our brave troops have pressed the enemy back and are now fighting valiantly on the holy earth of our motherland.

Now is the time to gird up your loins again. You have generously given me men, money and material. But my demand does not end here. Freedom cannot be achieved just by men, money and material. All we need is power of motive to ignite us to heroic deeds and valiant measures.

It will be a big folly if you think that you will live to see India free only because victory can now be achieved. None of you should have any wish to be alive to see your motherland free of enemy. A long fight still awaits us.

All of us should be having the sole desire to die to make our country breather. We should imbibe the desire to embrace a martyr's death. The path to freedom can be paved only by a martyr's blood.

My friends in the war of liberation! Today I have a sole and foremost demand from you all. Today, I demand of your blood. It is only blood that can help us take revenge of the blood that the British have scattered in our motherland. Only blood can pay the price of freedom.

Give me blood and I promise you freedom!

Madame Bhikaji Cama

Nationalist and Revolutionary

Born: 24th September, 1861
Died: 13th August, 1936

When Indian freedom fighters were fighting against the British in India, it became necessary for the world to know about the British tyranny. At this time, a brave and patriotic woman named Madame Bhikaji Cama took the responsibility of spreading India's cause in the world outside India.

Born in 1861 in a rich Parsi family, Madame Bhikaji Cama was a born nationalist and revolutionary. For 35 years, she created awareness in the whole of Europe about British India's pains and troubles. She urged the international community to come forward and unite to emancipate India from the clutches of the British domination. She also helped publish a magazine called 'Vande Mataram' to echo her nationalistic views.

A fearless lady, she is best known for her speech at the International Socialist Congress in Stuttgart, Germany, where she dynamically spoke out the condition of British India. She unfurled the Indian flag at the conference, which resembled the present day Indian flag. But it had the sun and moon, representing the unity and presence of Hindus and Muslims. Her speech received backlash from the British delegation but enormously helped in advocating India's cause.

British Tyranny in India

Friends, comrades and socialists, I have come here to speak for the dumb millions of Indians, who are going through terrible tyranny under the British government. You cannot dream of the poverty in that far-distant land, where the average income per head comes to three farthings a day – three farthings a day! Tell me, what other country can you compare with this? In no other part of the world such things exist. You will naturally ask me what is the cause of such poverty. My reply is that it is because thirty-five million pounds sterling are taken out of the land every year. Yes, it is entirely taken out because it goes to England to make that wealthy country more and more wealthy. While in India, owing to the poverty, we die half a million every month, and India means one-fifth of the human race. When I speak to you, I plead at the bar of humanity.

Brothers and sisters, take up the cause of justice and make it a point to bring India in front of every socialist Congress. Do not wait for representation from India. People oppressed as much as the Indians cannot do anything of that sort. How can they start representation in the land where liberty does not exist? That land whose very life is sucked by England by taking away thirty-five million pounds every year. Friends, take up this cause, whether or not the Indians are present at your Congress.

Let me tell you the truth that India's sufferings are greater. You must pass resolutions for India at every Congress. I only ask for moral support. We will fight for our rights ourselves. You must say that you are against the tyrannical and capitalist English. Say that you are for the sufferings for the millions of Indians.

I unfold this little flag before you friends, and I ask you in the name of the Indian nation to fight for justice. I wave this Indian national flag before you once again, and before concluding, let me tell you that I have every hope of seeking the Republic of India established during my lifetime.

OO

Patriotic Speeches from Around the World

Patrick Henry

American Revolutionary

Born: 29th May, 1736
Died: 6th June, 1799

In the history of orators and patriots, Patrick Henry will always remain an immortal name. An American revolutionary leader born on May 29, 1736, Henry was a successful lawyer and became immensely famous for his exceptional oratorical skills. He helped to make the first constitution of the state. Later, he served as governor. He was also a supporter of President George Washington and played a major role in the adoption of the Bill of Rights.

It was in 1775, at a Virginia assembly that he delivered his famous speech in defence of liberty, which concluded with the famous words "Give me liberty or give me death." In the speech, he urged for liberty and rights. This dynamic speech is still very famous amongst Americans and global citizens.

Give Me Liberty Or Give Me Death

No man thinks more highly than I do of the patriotism, as well as abilities, of the very worthy gentlemen, who have just addressed the House. But different men often see the same subject in different lights; and, therefore, I hope it will not be thought disrespectful to those gentlemen if, entertaining as I do opinions of a character very opposite to theirs, I shall speak forth my sentiments freely and without reserve. This is no time for ceremony. The question before the House is one of awful moment to this country. For my own part, I consider it as nothing less than a question of freedom or slavery; and in proportion to the magnitude of the subject ought to be the freedom of the debate. It is only in this way that we can hope to arrive at truth, and fulfil the great responsibility which we hold to God and our country. Should I keep back my opinions at such a time, through fear of giving offence, I should consider myself as guilty of treason towards my country, and of an act of disloyalty toward the Majesty of Heaven, which I revere above all earthly kings.

Mr. President, it is natural to man to indulge in the illusions of hope. We are apt to shut our eyes against a painful truth, and listen to the song of that siren till she transforms us into beasts. Is this the part of wise men, engaged in a great and arduous struggle for liberty? Are we disposed to be of the number of those who, having eyes, see not, and, having ears, hear not, the things which so nearly concern their temporal salvation? For my part, whatever anguish of spirit it may cost, I am willing to know the whole truth; to know the worst, and to provide for it.

I have but one lamp by which my feet are guided, and that is the lamp of experience. I know of no way of judging of the future but by the past. And judging by the past, I wish to know what there has been in the conduct of the British ministry for the last ten years to justify those hopes with which gentlemen have been pleased to solace themselves and the House. Is it that insidious smile with which our petition has been lately received? Trust it not, sir; it will prove a snare to your feet. Suffer not yourselves to be betrayed with a kiss. Ask yourselves how this gracious reception of our petition comports with those warlike preparations which cover our waters and darken our land. Are fleets and armies necessary to a work of love and reconciliation? Have we shown ourselves so unwilling to be reconciled that force must be called in to win back our love? Let us not deceive ourselves, sir. These are the implements of war and subjugation; the last arguments to which kings resort.

I ask gentlemen, sir, what means this martial array, if its purpose be not to force us to submission? Can gentlemen assign any other possible motive for it? Has Great Britain any enemy, in this quarter of the world, to call for all this accumulation of navies and armies? No, sir, she has none. They are meant for us: they can be meant for no other. They are sent over to bind and rivet upon us, those chains which the British ministry have been so long forging. And what have we to oppose to them? Shall we try argument? Sir, we have been trying that for the last ten years. Have we anything new to offer upon the subject? Nothing. We have held the subject up in every light of which it is capable; but it has been all in vain. Shall we resort to entreaty and humble supplication? What terms shall we find which have not been already exhausted? Let us not, I beseech you, sir, deceive ourselves. Sir, we have done everything that could be done to avert the storm which is now coming on. We have petitioned; we have remonstrated; we have supplicated; we have prostrated ourselves before the throne, and have implored its interposition to arrest the tyrannical hands of the ministry and parliament. Our petitions have been slighted; our remonstrances have produced additional violence and insult; our supplications have been disregarded; and we have been spurned, with contempt, from the foot of the throne! In vain, after these things, may we indulge in the fond hope of peace and reconciliation. There is no longer any room for hope. If we wish to be free – if we mean to preserve and inviolate those inestimable privileges for which we have been so long contending – if we mean not basely to abandon the noble struggle in which we have been so long engaged, and which we have pledged ourselves never to abandon until the glorious object of our contest shall be obtained – we must fight! I repeat it, sir, we must fight! An appeal to arms and to the God of hosts is all that is left us!

They tell us, sir, that we are weak; unable to cope with so formidable an adversary. But when shall we be stronger? Will it be the next week, or the next year? Will it be when we are totally disarmed, and when a British guard shall be stationed in every house? Shall we gather strength by irresolution and inaction? Shall we acquire the means of effectual resistance by lying on our backs and hugging the phantom of hope, until our enemies shall have bound us hand and foot? Sir, we are not weak if we make a proper use of those means which the God of nature hath placed in our power. The millions of people, armed in the holy cause of liberty, and in such a country as that which we possess, are invincible by any force which our enemy can send against us. Besides, sir, we shall not fight our battles alone. There is a just God, who presides over the destinies of nations, and who will raise up friends to fight our battles for us. The battle, sir, is not to the strong alone; it is to the vigilant, the active, the brave. Besides, sir, we have no election. If we were base enough to desire it, it is now too late to retire from the contest. There is no retreat but in submission and slavery! Our chains are forged! Their clanking may be heard on the plains of Boston! The war is inevitable – and let it come! I repeat it, sir, let it come.

It is in vain, sir, to extenuate the matter. Gentlemen may cry, Peace, Peace – but there is no peace. The war is actually begun! The next gale that sweeps from the north will bring to our ears the clash of resounding arms! Our brethren are already in the field! Why stand we here idle? What is it that gentlemen wish? What would they have? Is life so dear, or peace so sweet, as to be purchased at the price of chains and slavery? Forbid it, Almighty God! I know not what course others may take; but as for me, give me liberty or give me death!

John F. Kennedy

Former Flamboyant President of the United States

Born: 29th May, 1917
Died: 22nd November, 1963

Born in 1917, John F. Kennedy remains as the most flamboyant president of the US. He was known for his charismatic personality and eloquent speeches that left many spellbound. He reformed the US and developed noble relations with the outside world.

He became the President of the US in 1961 and delivered a heartwarming speech in his inaugural address. He called Americans to "ask not what your country can do for you, ask what you can do for your country." He also emphasised on having good relations with other countries, and urged Americans to rise and work.

Ask not what your country can do for you...

Vice President Johnson, Mr. Speaker, Mr. Chief Justice, President Eisenhower, Vice President Nixon, President Truman, Reverend Clergy, fellow citizens:

We observe today not a victory of party but a celebration of freedom – symbolising an end as well as a beginning – signifying renewal as well as change. For I have sworn before you and Almighty God the same oath our forbears prescribed nearly a century and three quarters ago.

The world is very different now. For man holds in his mortal hands, the power to abolish all forms of human poverty and all forms of human life. And yet, the same revolutionary beliefs for which our forebears fought are still at issue around the globe — the belief that the rights of man come not from the generosity of the state but from the hand of God.

Let every nation know, whether it wishes us well or ill, that we shall pay any price, bear any burden, meet any hardship, support any friend, oppose any foe to assure the survival and the success of liberty.

This much we pledge — and more.

To those old allies whose cultural and spiritual origins we share, we pledge the loyalty of faithful friends. United there is little, we cannot do in a host of cooperative ventures. Divided there is little we can do — for we dare not meet a powerful challenge at odds and split asunder.

To those people in the huts and villages of half the globe struggling to break the bonds of mass misery, we pledge our best efforts to help them help themselves, for whatever period is required — not because the communists may be doing it, not because we seek their votes, but because it is right. If a free society cannot help the many, who are poor, it cannot save the few, who are rich.

So let us begin anew — remembering on both sides that civility is not a sign of weakness, and sincerity is always subject to proof. Let us never negotiate out of fear. But let us never fear to negotiate.

Let both sides explore what problems unite us instead of belabouring those problems which divide us.

Let both sides, for the first time, formulate serious and precise proposals for the inspection and control of arms – and bring the absolute power to destroy other nations under the absolute control of all nations.

Let both sides seek to invoke the wonders of science instead of its terrors. Together let us explore the stars, conquer the deserts, eradicate disease, tap the ocean depths and encourage the arts and commerce.

Let both sides unite to heed in all corners of the earth the command of **Isaiah** – to "undo the heavy burdens . . . (and) let the oppressed go free."

And if a beachhead of cooperation may push back the jungle of suspicion, let both sides join in creating a new endeavour, not a new balance of power, but a new world of law, where the strong are just and the weak secure and the peace preserved.

All this will not be finished in the first one hundred days. Nor will it be finished in the first one thousand days, nor in the life of this administration, nor even perhaps in our lifetime on this planet. But let us begin.

In your hands, my fellow citizens, more than mine, will rest the final success or failure of our course. Since this country was founded, each generation of Americans has been summoned to give testimony to its national loyalty. The graves of young Americans, who answered the call to service surround the globe.

In the long history of the world, only a few generations have been granted the role of defending freedom in its hour of maximum danger. I do not shrink from this responsibility – I welcome it. I do not believe that any of us would exchange places with any other people or any other generation. The energy, the faith, the devotion which we bring to this endeavour will light our country and all, who serve it – and the glow from that fire can truly light the world.

And so, my fellow Americans: ask not what your country can do for you – ask what you can do for your country.

My fellow citizens of the world: ask not what America will do for you, but what together we can do for the freedom of man.

With a good conscience our only sure reward, with history the final judge of our deeds, let us go forth to lead the land we love, asking His blessing and His help, but knowing that here on earth, God's work must truly be our own.

OO

Sardar Vallabhbhai Patel

The Iron Man of India

Born: 31st October, 1875

Died: 15th December, 1950

Sardar Patel, born in 1875, remains as a famous freedom fighter and India's best Home Minister till date. He was a very close associate of Mahatma Gandhi. He is popularly known as the 'Iron Man of India' for his strong resolution to bring together the scattered princely states of India. When the British left, India was scattered into more than 500 small princely states. It was a difficult task to bring them close and make them join the Constitution. It was Sardar Patel, who achieved this task. With his shrewd and persuasive nature, he integrated these states into India.

After India achieved independence, Sardar Patel became India's first Deputy Prime Minister while Jawaharlal Nehru became the first Prime Minister. Sardar also held the posts of Home Minister and Information & Broadcasting Minister. He not only helped unite these states of India, but also vigorously worked for the rehabilitation of the refugees of India-Pakistan Partition.

The following speech was delivered by Sardar Patel after he took charge of the department set up especially for integrating the Indian states. This speech was delivered on July 3, 1947.

A United India

A few days back, it was announced that the Indian Government had decided to create a department that would deal with the relationship with the states. This department has been founded and the states also know that. On this significant day, I would like to state a few points to my friends, the rulers of these states.

We have to learn a lesson from history. India has been fragmented and not united and that is the reason why many invaders have been able to conquer our land. Our mutual conflicts and fights have allowed foreign powers to conquer our land many times. We must not repeat our mistakes to lose our independence again. We are just a step away from our independence. I acknowledge the fact that we have been unable to keep the unity of our country unimpaired in the final phase. Many of us have been disappointed and grieved by the fact that some parts have gone out of India to form their own governments. However, it is true that common cultures and traditions will rule us despite this separation. This would be true with several states that would continue to have congenial relationship and cooperation with the rest of India due to their unbreakable ties – economic, cultural and political. For safety and survival of these states and India, it is necessary to be mutually friendly and be united.

The British created the doctrine of paramountcy when they began their rule in India. This doctrine only served the interests of the British. The doctrine has been more of subordination than cooperation. If we ignore the area of paramountcy, we will be able to see that there is a broad sphere in which the relations between these states and British India have flourished because of mutual benefits. A demand is being echoed that these states should now be independent, as the British are leaving India. I have deep sympathy with the Indian states but I think they do not advocate a freedom that may be harmful to the unity and welfare of India. Those states that have joined the Constituent Assembly have already shown that they certainly want welfare and unity in India. I appeal to the other states to walk on the same footsteps too. I request them to join the Constituent Assembly.

India and its Constitution belong to the citizens of the country. We are all one because of the same blood and feelings we share. No one can break us into fragments and no obstacles can be created between us. Therefore, I believe that we should, like friends, sit together and make laws than create treaties as separate entities. I have an invitation for all, the rulers of the states, my friends, to come to the councils of the Constituent Assembly in this congenial spirit and which will also be for the common good for us.

I believe that there is some misunderstanding about the attitude of the Congress towards the states. Hereupon, I will make it clear that the Congress does not wish to interfere in the internal affairs of the states. However, under this aegis, the Congress wishes the states satisfaction, wealth and joy. I do not advocate any policy under the new department that would state control of power of one state by the other. If there be any control that would be of mutual benefit and development. Hereby, I suggest to look at the option of combining with the administration of the new department, a Standing Committee representative of British India and the states.

We stand at a crucial juncture of the Indian history. If we hold hands, we can take our country to newer heights, but if we do not stand united, we fall to greater depths. I believe that the Indian states will understand that their opposition to cooperation will be termed 'anarchy' and 'chaos'. We will be cursed by the posterity if we fail to transform this situation into mutual advantage. Let us come together to place this sacred motherland of ours at the right place among the nations of the world and transform it into a place of peace and development.

Dr. A.P.J. Abdul Kalam

Father of India's Missile Programme/President of India

Born: 15th October, 1931

Dr. A.P.J. Abdul Kalam is the 11th President of India and a renowned scientist. Ever since, he has become the President, he has urged the youth of India to embrace nationalism and work together in the making of a developed India.

Born on October 15, 1931, Dr. Kalam developed India's first Satellite Launch Vehicle (SLV-III). He also developed Agni and Prithvi Missiles and was the brain behind the Pokhran-II nuclear tests. He has also worked at ISRO and DRDO.

As the President of India, Dr. Kalam aims to make India a developed country by 2020. He constantly calls on the youth to work towards the progress of the nation. In the following speech, he gives an important social message to all the Indians, urging them to transform India from a developing nation to a developed nation.

Vision for India

I have three visions for India. In 3000 years of our history, people from all over the world have come and invaded us, captured our lands, conquered our minds. From Alexander onwards, the Greeks, the Turks, the Moguls, the Portuguese, the British, the French, the Dutch, all of them came and looted us, took over what was ours. Yet we have not done this to any other nation. We have not conquered anyone. We have not grabbed their land, their culture, their history and tried to enforce our way of life on them. Why? Because we respect the freedom of others. That is why my first vision is that of FREEDOM. I believe that India got its first vision of this in 1857, when we started the war of independence. It is this freedom that we must protect and nurture and build on. If we are not free, no one will respect us.

My second vision for India is DEVELOPMENT. For fifty years, we have been a developing nation. It is time, we see ourselves as a developed nation. We are among top five nations of the world in terms of GDP. We have 10 per cent growth rate in most areas. Our poverty levels are falling. Our achievements are being globally recognised today. Yet we lack the self-confidence to see ourselves as a developed nation, self-reliant and self-assured. Isn't this incorrect?

I have a third vision. India must stand up to the world. Because I believe that unless India stands up to the world, no one will respect us. Only strength respects strength. We must be strong not only as a military power but also as an economic power. Both must go hand-in-hand.

I see four milestones in my career:

One: Twenty years I spent in ISRO. I was given the opportunity to be the project director for India's first satellite launch vehicle, (SLV III). The one that launched *Rohini.* These years played a very important role in my life of a scientist.

Two: After my ISRO years, I joined DRDO and got a chance to be the part of India's missile program. It was my second bliss when *Agni* met its mission requirements in 1994.

Three: The Department of Atomic Energy and DRDO had this tremendous partnership in the recent nuclear tests, on May 11 and 13. This was the third bliss.The joy of participating with my team in these nuclear tests and proving to the world that India can make it, that we are no longer a developing nation but one of them. It made me feel very proud as an Indian. The fact that we have now developed for *Agni* a re-entry structure, for which we have developed this new material. A very light material called **carbon-carbon**.

Four: One day an orthopaedic surgeon from Nizam Institute of Medical Sciences visited my laboratory. He lifted the material and found it so light that he took me to his hospital and showed me his patients. There were these little girls and boys with heavy metallic calipers weighing over three kgs. each, dragging their feet around. He said to me: Please remove the pain of my patients. In three weeks, we made these Floor Reaction Orthosis 300 gram calipers and took them to the orthopaedic centre. The children didn't believe their eyes. From dragging around a three kg. load on their legs, they could now move around! Their parents had tears in their eyes. That was my fourth bliss!

Why is the media here so negative? Why are we in India so embarrassed to recognise our own strengths, our achievements? We are such a great nation. We have so many amazing success stories but we refuse to acknowledge them. Why? We are the first in milk production. We are number one in Remote Sensing Satellites. We are the second largest producer of wheat. We are the second largest producer of rice. Look at Dr. Sudarshan, he has transferred the tribal village into a self-sustaining, self-driving unit. There are millions of such achievements but our media is only obsessed in the bad news and failures and disasters.

I was in Tel Aviv once and I was reading the Israeli newspaper. It was the day after a lot of attacks, bombardments and deaths that had taken place. But the front page of the newspaper had the picture of a Jewish gentleman, who in five years had transformed his desert land into an orchid and a granary. It was this inspiring picture that everyone woke up to. The gory details of killings, bombardments, deaths, were inside in the newspaper, buried among other news. In India, we only read about death, sickness, terrorism, crime. Why are we so negative? Another question: Why are we, as a nation so obsessed with foreign things? We want foreign TVs, we want foreign shirts. We want foreign technology. Why this obsession with everything imported. Do we not realise that self-respect comes with self-reliance?

I was in Hyderabad giving this lecture, when a 14-year-old girl asked me for my autograph. I asked her what her goal in life is: She replied: I want to live in a developed India. For her, you and I will have to build this developed India. You must proclaim. India is not an under-developed nation; it is a highly developed nation.

Allow me to come back with vengeance. Got 10 minutes for your country?

You say that our government is inefficient. You say that our laws are too old. You say that the municipality does not pick up the garbage. You say that the phones don't work, the railways are a joke, the airline is the worst in the world, mails never reach their destination. You say that our country has been fed to the dogs and is in the absolute pits. You say, say and say.

What do You do about it? Take a person on his way to Singapore. Give him a name – Yours. Give him a face – Yours. You walk out of the airport and you are at your

International best. In Singapore, you don't throw cigarette butts on the roads or eat in the stores. You are as proud of their Underground Links as they are. You pay $5 (approx. Rs. 60) to drive through Orchard Road (equivalent of Mahim Causeway or Pedder Road) between 5 PM and 8 PM.

You comeback to the parking lot to punch your parking ticket if you have overstayed in a restaurant or a shopping mall irrespective of your status identity. In Singapore, you don't say anything, Do you? You wouldn't dare to eat in public during Ramadan, in Dubai. You would not dare to go out without your head covered in Jeddah. You would not dare to buy an employee of the telephone exchange in London at 10 pounds (Rs. 650) a month to see to it that my STD and ISD calls are billed to someone else. YOU would not dare to speed beyond 55 mph (88 kph) in Washington and then tell the traffic cop, *"Jaanta hai main kaun hoon* (Do you know who I am?). I am so and so's son. Take your two bucks and get lost."* You wouldn't chuck an empty coconut shell anywhere other than the garbage pail on the beaches in Australia and New Zealand. Why don't you spit *paan* on the streets of Tokyo? Why don't you use examination jockeys or buy fake certificates in Boston? We are still talking of the same you. You, who can respect and conform to a foreign system in other countries, but cannot in your own. You, who will throw papers and cigarettes on the road, the moment, you touch Indian ground. If you can be an involved and appreciative citizen in an alien country, why cannot you be the same here in India.

Once in an interview, the famous Ex-municipal commissioner of Mumbai, Mr. Tinaikar had a point to make. "Rich people's dogs are walked on the streets to leave their affluent droppings all over the place," he said. "And then the same people turn around to criticise and blame the authorities for inefficiency and dirty pavements. What do they expect the officers to do? Go down with a broom every time their dog feels the pressure in his bowels? In America, every dog owner has to clean up after his pet has done the job. Same in Japan. Will the Indian citizen do that here?" He's right. We go to the polls to choose a government and after that forfeit all responsibility. We sit back wanting to be pampered and expect the government to do everything for us whilst our contribution is totally negative. We expect the government to clean up but we are not going to stop chucking garbage all over the place nor are we going to stop to pick up a stray piece of paper and throw it in the bin. We expect the railways to provide clean bathrooms but we are not going to learn the proper use of bathrooms. We want Indian Airlines and Air India to provide the best of food and toiletries but we are not going to stop pilfering at the least opportunity. This applies even to the staff, who is known not to pass on the service to the public.

When it comes to burning social issues like those related to women, dowry, girl-child and others, we make loud drawing room protestation and continue to do the reverse at home. Our excuse? "It's the whole system which has to change, how will it matter if I alone forego my sons' rights to a dowry." So who's going to change the system? What does a system consist of? Very conveniently, for us it consists of our neighbours, other households, other cities, other communities and the government. But definitely, not me and you. When it comes to us actually making a positive contribution to the system, we lock ourselves along with our families into a safe cocoon and look into the distance at countries far away and wait for a Mr. Clean to come along and work miracles for us with a majestic sweep of his hand. Or we leave the country and run away. Like lazy cowards hounded by our fears, we run to America to bask in their glory and praise their system. When New York becomes insecure, we run to England. When England experiences unemployment, we take the next flight out to the Gulf. When the Gulf is war-struck, we demand to be rescued and brought home by the Indian government. Everybody is out to abuse and rape the country. Nobody thinks of feeding the system. Our conscience is mortgaged to money.

Eamon de Valera

Irish Revolutionary Leader and Statesman

Born: 14th October, 1882
Died: 29th August, 1975

Eamon de Valera, one of the greatest patriots world has ever seen, was born in 1882 and went to become a dynamic Irish Prime Minister. Valera is perhaps, the most important person to have been born in Ireland. He served as prime minister from 1932 to 1948, and made his country, a sovereign state. He became the President of Ireland in 1959 and served till 1973. His glorious and famous life came to an end in 1975 in Dublin in Ireland.

Valera was an orator of exceptional excellence. His addresses to the nation influenced many. In his many speeches, he talked about the glory of Ireland and inspired people to keep intact the traditions and values of Ireland. Following is one of his speeches delivered on February 6, 1933, in which he talks about the spiritual, literary and unique wealth of Ireland.

Ireland Among the Nations

Ireland has much to seek from the rest of the world, and much to give back in return. Much that she alone can give. Her gifts are the fruit of special qualities of mind and heart, developed by centuries of eventful history. Alone among the countries of Western Europe, she never came under sway of

Imperial Rome. When all her neighbouring countries were conquered, she remained unconquered, creating her own civilisation.

Ireland's greatest contribution to the welfare of humanity has been the example of devotion to freedom which she has given throughout since hundred years. The invaders, who came to Ireland in the 12th century belonged to a race that had already defeated England and many other countries in Europe. It was only in Ireland that they met most serious resistance – a resistance which was seen generations after generations and will incessantly continue until the last sod in the soil is freed.

The Irish language is one of the oldest, and from the point of view of the philologist, one of the most interesting in Europe. It is a member of the Indo-European family, and closely related to Greek and Sanskrit, and still more closely related to Latin.

The tradition of Irish learning was not even lost during the darkest period of the English occupation. Irish education has always been kept alive in colleges of Louvain, Rome, Salamanca, Paris and many other parts of Europe. In Ireland itself, the schools of poetry survived in some places until the beginning of the eighteenth century, maintaining to the end their rigorous discipline.

Ireland has produced in Dean Swift perhaps, the greatest satirist in the English language; in Edmund Burke probably, the greatest writer on politics; in William Carleton, a novelist of first rank; in Oliver Goldsmith, a poet of rare merit. Henry Grattan was one of the most eloquent orators of his time – the golden age of oratory in the English language. Theobald Wolfe has left us with one of the most delightful autobiographies in literature. Several recent or still living

Irish novelists and poets have produced work which is likely to stand the test of time. The Irish theatre movement has given us the finest school of acting of the present day, and some plays of high quality.

I have spoken at some length of Ireland's history and her contributions to European culture, because I wish to emphasise that what Ireland has done in the past, she can do in the future. The Irish genius has always stressed spiritual and intellectual rather than material values. That is the characterisation that fits the Irish people in the special manner for the task of saving the Western civilisation.

Inspiring Speeches
During Wars

Winston Churchill

Former Prime Minister of England and a Prolific Writer

Born: 30th November, 1874

Died: 24th January, 1965

Winston Churchill was a great personality, who possessed numerous talents and skills. He was a statesman, writer and politician of the highest quality. He is best known for his inspiring speeches that he delivered when England was fighting World War II.

He was the Prime Minister (1940-45) of England when World War II was going on. England joined the conglomerate of the Soviet Union and USA to battle against German dictator Adolf Hitler. He encouraged his forces to fight bravely and think only of victory, and his inspiration was so effective that his forces fought with determination and won the war. Winston Churchill was also a renowned writer and he won the Nobel Prize for Literature in 1953.

Winston Churchill was elected as Prime Minister of England on May 10, 1940 and he delivered on May 13, 1940, a mind-blowing speech that was praised by leaders across the globe. In the speech titled 'Blood, toil, tears and sweat', Churchill urged everyone seated in the parliament to go for just victory against all odds.

Blood, Toil, Tears and Sweat

I beg to move, that this House welcomes the formation of a Government representing the united and inflexible resolve of the nation to prosecute the war with Germany to a victorious conclusion. I have completed the most important part of this task. A War Cabinet has been formed of five members, representing, with the Opposition Liberals, the unity of the nation. The three party Leaders have agreed to serve, either in the War Cabinet or in high executive office. The three Fighting Services have been filled. It was necessary that this should be done in one single day, on account of the extreme urgency and rigour of events. A number of other positions, key positions, were filled yesterday, and I am submitting a further list to His Majesty tonight. I hope to complete the appointment of the principal Ministers during tomorrow. The appointment of the other Ministers usually takes a little longer, but I trust that, when Parliament meets again, this part of my task will be completed, and that the administration will be complete in all respects.

I now invite the House to record its approval of the steps taken and to declare its confidence in the new Government. To form an administration of this scale and complexity is a serious undertaking in itself, but it must be remembered that we are in the preliminary stage of one of the greatest battles in history, that we are in action at many other points in Norway and in Holland, that we have to be prepared in the Mediterranean, that the air battle is continuous and that many preparations. In this crisis, I hope I may be pardoned if I do not address the House at any length today. I hope that any of my friends and colleagues, or former colleagues, who are affected by the political reconstruction, will make allowance, all allowance, for any lack of ceremony with which it has been necessary to act. I would say to the House, as I said to those, who have joined this government: "I have nothing to offer but blood, toil, tears and sweat."

We have before us an ordeal of the most grievous kind. We have before us many, many long months of struggle and of suffering. You ask, what is our policy? I can say: It is to wage war, by sea, land and air, with all our might and with all the strength that God can give us; to wage war against a monstrous tyranny, never surpassed in the dark, lamentable catalogue of human crime. That is our policy. You ask, what is our aim? I can answer in one word: It is victory, victory at all costs, victory inspite of all terror, victory, however, long and hard the road may be; for without victory, there is no survival. Let that be realised; no survival for the British Empire, no survival for all that the British Empire has stood for, no survival for the urge and impulse of the ages, that mankind will move forward towards its goal. But I take up my task with buoyancy and hope. I feel sure that our cause will not be suffered to fail among men. At this time, I feel entitled to claim the aid of all, and I say, "come then, let us go forward together with our united strength."

Napoleon Bonaparte

French Emperor and General

Born: 15th August, 1769
Died: 5th May, 1821

Lean and skinny in stature, Napoleon still remains as the most intimidating generals in the history of world military. Born in Italy on August 15, 1769, he became an army officer in 1785, and was a military dictator in 1799. He led his forces remarkably well to win battles in Europe and Russia. His powerful dictatorship lasted till 1815 when he was defeated in the Battle of Waterloo. Napoleon was the master of his words and it was the everlasting effect of his inspirational speeches to his soldiers that lead him to numerous victories.

Following are few of his selected speeches:

Before the war against Italy (27th March, 1796)

"Soldiers, you are naked and undernourished. The government owes you much, but can give you nothing. Your patience in bearing all privations and your courage in facing all kinds of danger have won the admiration of France. She is a witness to your hardships. You have no shoes or coats or shirts, and almost no food. It is up to you to capture them. You want to do it, and you can do it. Let's go!

On entering Milan (30th May, 1796)

"Soldiers, You have rushed like a torrent from the top of the Apennines; you have overthrown and scattered all that opposed your march. Milan is yours, and the republican flag waves throughout Lombarty. The dukes of Parma and Modena own their political existence to your generosity alone. The army which so proudly threatened you can find no barrier to protect it against your courage, neither the Po, the Ticino, nor the Adda could stop you for a single day. These vaunted bulwarks of Italy opposed in vain; you passed them as rapidly as the Apennines.

These great successes have filled the heart of your country with joy. Your representatives have ordered a festival to commemorate your victories, which has been held in every district of the republic. There your fathers, your mothers, your wives and sisters rejoiced in your good fortune and proudly boasted of belonging to you.

Yes, soldiers you have done much – but remains there nothing more to do? Shall it be said of us that we knew how to conquer, but not how to make use of victory?

But I see you already hasten to arms. An effeminate repose is tedious to you: the days which are lost to glory are lost to your happiness. Well, then, let us set forth.

On the beginning of the Russian Campaign (1812)

Soldiers, the second war of Poland has begun. At Tilsit, Russia swore eternal alliance with France and war with England. She has openly violated her oath, and refuses to offer any explanation of her strange conduct. Russia is impelled onward by fatality. Her destiny is about to be accomplished. Does she believe that we have degenerated? She has been placed between dishonour and war. The choice cannot for an instant be doubtful.

Let us march forward, then, and crossing the Niemen, carry the war into her territories. The second war of Poland will be to the French army as glorious as the first. But our next peace must carry with its guaranty and put an end to that arrogant influence which for last fifty years Russia has exercised over the affairs of Europe.

Farewell to the old guard (20th April, 1814)

Soldiers of my old guard, I bid you farewell. For twenty years, I have constantly accompanied you on the road to honour and glory. In these latter times, as in the days of our prosperity, you have invariably been models of courage and fidelity. With men such as you are our cause could not be lost. But the war would have been interminable, it would have been civil war, and that could have entailed deeper misfortunes on France. I have sacrificed all my interests to those of the country.

I go, but you, my friends, will continue to serve France. Her happiness was only my thought. It will still be the object of my wishes. Do not regret my fate. If I have consented to survive, it is to serve your glory. I intend to write the history of the great achievements, we have performed together. Adieum, my friends. I wish could press you all to my heart.

OO

Joseph Stalin

Russian Communist Leader

Born: 21ˢᵗ December, 1879

Died: 5ᵗʰ March, 1953

Born in 1879, Joseph Stalin was the head of the Soviet Union and disciple of a famous teacher, Lenin. It is learnt that Joseph Stalin was the son of a cobbler. He was sent to the local church school from where he was expelled at the age of 15 due to his revolutionary activities. He reformed the Soviet Union and introduced five-year plans. He ruled Soviet Union in an important period as they had to fight in the World War II during his regime. He turned Soviet Union into a military power after the World War.

When the German forces attacked Soviet Union, they managed to conquer parts of Soviet Union in the early stages. On July 3, 1941, Joseph Stalin revived the demoralised spirits of his countrymen through his dynamic address, urging them to fight "till the last drop of our blood."

Comrades! Citizens! Brothers and Sisters! Men of our army and navy! I am addressing you, my friends! The perfidious military attack on our Fatherland, begun on June 22nd by Hitler Germany, is continuing.

Inspite of the heroic resistance of the Red Army, and although the enemy's finest divisions and finest air force units have already been smashed and have met their doom on the field of battle, the enemy continues to push forward, hurling fresh forces into the attack.

Hitler's troops have succeeded in capturing Lithuania, a considerable part of Latvia, the western part of Byelo-Russia, part of Western Ukraine, and is bombing Murmansk, Orsha, Mogilev, Smolensk, Kiev, Odessa and Sebastopol.

A grave danger hangs over our country.

How could it have happened that our glorious Red Army surrendered a number of our cities and districts to fascist armies? Is it really true that German fascist troops are invincible, as is ceaselessly trumpeted by the boastful fascist propagandists? Of course, not!

History shows that there are no invincible armies and never have been. Napoleon's army was considered invincible but it was beaten successively by Russian, English and German armies. The same must be said of Hitler's German fascist army today. This army had not yet met with serious resistance on the continent of Europe. Only on our territory has it met serious resistance. And if, as a result of this resistance, the finest divisions of Hitler's German fascist army have been defeated by our Red Army, it means that this army too can be smashed and will be smashed.

As to part of our territory having nevertheless been seized by German fascist troops, this is chiefly due to the fact that the war of fascist Germany on the USSR began under conditions favourable for the German forces and unfavourable for the Soviet forces. She has gained a certain advantageous position for her troops for a short period, but she has lost politically by exposing herself in the eyes of the entire world as a blood-thirsty aggressor.

Our whole valiant Red Army, our whole valiant Navy, all our falcons of the air, all the peoples of our country, all the finest men and women of Europe, America and Asia, finally all the finest men and women of Germany – condemn the treacherous acts of German fascists and sympathise with the Soviet Government, approve the conduct of the Soviet Government, and see that ours is a just cause, that the enemy will be defeated, that we are bound to win.

Our troops are fighting heroically against an enemy armed to the teeth with tanks and aircraft. Overcoming innumerable difficulties, the Red Army and Red Navy are self-sacrificingly disputing every inch of the Soviet soil. The main forces of the Red Army are coming into action armed with thousands of tanks and aeroplanes. The men of the Red Army are displaying unexampled valour. Our resistance to the enemy is growing in strength and power. Side by side with the Red Army, the entire Soviet people are rising in defence of our native land.

The enemy is cruel and implacable. He is out to seize our lands, watered with our sweat, to seize our grain and oil secured by our labour. He is out to restore the rule of landlords, to destroy national culture and the national state existence of the citizens of USSR, to convert them into the slaves of German princes and barons. The Soviet people must abandon all heedlessness, they must mobilise themselves and reorganise all their work on new, wartime bases, when there can be no mercy to the enemy.

Further, there must be no room in our ranks for cowards and deserters. Our people must know no fear in fight and must selflessly join our patriotic war of liberation, our war against the fascist enslavers. All our work must be immediately reconstructed on a war footing, everything must be subordinated to the interests of the front and the task of organising the demolition of the enemy.

The people of the Soviet Union must rise against the enemy and defend their rights and their land. The Red Army, Red Navy and all citizens of the Soviet Union must defend every inch of the Soviet soil, must fight to the last drop of blood for our towns and villages, must display the daring initiative and intelligence that are inherent in our people. We must organise all-round assistance for the Red Army, ensure powerful reinforcements for its ranks and the supply of everything it requires. We must organise the rapid transport of troops and military freight and extensive aid to the wounded. All our industries got to work with greater intensity to produce more rifles, machine-guns, artillery, bullets, shells, airplanes. We must organise the guarding of factories, power-stations, telephonic and telegraphic communications and arrange effective air raid precautions in all localities.

We must bear in mind that the enemy is crafty, unscrupulous, experienced in deception and the dissemination of false rumours. The collective farmers must drive off all their cattle, and turn over their grain to the safe-keeping of State authorities for transportation to the rear. All valuable property, including non-ferrous metals, grain and fuel which cannot be withdrawn, must without fail be destroyed.

Comrades, our forces are numberless. The overweening enemy will soon learn this to his cost. Side by side with the Red Army many thousands of workers, collective farmers, intellectuals are rising to fight the enemy aggressor. The masses of our people will rise up in their millions.

All our forces for support of our heroic Red Army and our glorious Red Navy! All forces of the people – for the demolition of the enemy!

Forward, to our victory!

OO

Abraham Lincoln

Emancipator of Slaves/Former President of the United States

Born: 12th February, 1809

Died: 14th April, 1865

Abraham Lincoln, the 16th President of the United States, was the US President in the 19th century and is widely considered to be the man, who changed the fate of the US. He remained the President of US (1861–65) and arguably the best orator, US has ever seen. He is still known for his shrewdness and honesty. In the 1860 presidential election, he won by a large margin in the electoral college.

When Lincoln was the President of the US, the American Civil War was going on. But Lincoln proved to be an excellent wartime leader. Lincoln was again elected as president in 1864 and he again won by a huge margin. On April 14, 1865, five days after the American Civil War ended, he was assassinated.

Among his many inspiring speeches and addresses to the nation, his Gettysburg Address on 19th November, 1863 is the most famous. This speech was delivered to the nation during the American Civil War when more than 45,000 men were killed. This speech was dedicated to those men. Though a very short speech, it had long-lasting influence on the whole of nation.

'Government of the people, by the people, for the people' – Gettysburg Address

Four score and seven years ago, our fathers brought forth on this continent, a new nation, conceived in Liberty, and dedicated to the proposition that all men are created equal.

Now we are engaged in a great civil war, testing whether that nation, or any nation so conceived and so dedicated, can long endure. We are met on a great battlefield of that war. We have come to dedicate a portion of that field, as a final resting place for those who, here gave their lives that the nation might live. It is altogether fitting and proper that we should do this.

But, in a larger sense, we cannot dedicate – we cannot consecrate – we cannot hallow – this ground. The brave men, living and dead, who struggled here, have consecrated it, far above our poor power to add or detract. The world will little note, nor long remember what we say here, but it can never forget what they did here. It is for us the living, rather, to be dedicated here to the unfinished work which they, who fought here have thus far so nobly advanced. It is rather for us to be here dedicated to the great task remaining before us – that from these honoured dead we take increased devotion to that cause for which they gave the last full measure of devotion – that we here highly resolve that these dead shall not have died in vain – that this nation, under God, shall have a new birth of freedom – and that government of the people, by the people, for the people, shall not perish from the earth.

∞

Speeches Against
Racial Discrimination

Nelson Mandela

Black Nationalist Leader/Former President of South Africa

Born: 18th July, 1918

Born on July 18, 1918, in South Africa, Nelson Mandela stands as the greatest epitome of apartheid struggle that suppressed the Blacks' rights for the better part of the 20th century. A leader and statesman of a class of his own, he struggled against the privileged white government and led many revolutions against them. He was arrested by the tyrannical White Government and sentenced to life imprisonment (twenty-seven years). Largely adored and followed by the people in South Africa, he is also a venerable personality throughout the world. In 1993, Mandela was awarded the Nobel Peace Prize and in 1994, he was elected the President of South Africa. He retired from public life in June 1999 and presently resides in his birth place, Ounu, Transkei.

When Mandela was released in 1990 from his life imprisonment, he received a rousing welcome by his followers and the international community. At this moment, on February 18, 1990, he delivered a heart-warming speech to his people asking them to come together and fight for the cause, he had sacrificed the life for. Apartheid was finally eradicated after a year Mandela delivered this speech.

Friends, Comrades and fellow South Africans!

I greet you all in the name of peace, democracy and freedom for all. I stand here before you not as a prophet but as a humble servant of you, the people. Your tireless and heroic sacrifices have made it possible for me to be here today. I therefore, place the remaining years of my life in your hands...

Today the majority of South Africans, black and white, recognise that apartheid has no future. It has to be ended by our own decisive mass action in order to build peace and security. The mass campaign of defiance and other actions of our organisation and people can only culminate in the establishment of democracy. The apartheid destruction in our sub-continent is incalculable. Millions are homeless and unemployed, our economy lies in the ruins and our people are embroiled in political strife.

Our resort to the armed struggle in 1960 with the formation of the military wing of the ANC, Umkhonto, We Sizwe (Spear of the Nation) was a purely defensive action against the violence of apartheid. The factor which necessitated the armed struggle still exists today. We have no option but to continue...

There must be an end to white monopoly on political power, and a fundamental restructuring of our political and economic systems to ensure that the inequities of apartheid are addressed and our society thoroughly democratised.

Our struggle received a decisive moment. We call on our people to seize this moment, so that the process towards democracy is rapid and uninterrupted.

We have waited too long for our freedom! We can no longer wait. Now is the time to intensify the struggle on all fronts. To relax our efforts now would be a mistake which generations to come will not be able to forgive. It is only through disciplined mass action that our victory can be assured.

We call our white compatriots to join us in the shaping of a new South Africa. We call on the international community to continue the campaign to isolate the apartheid regime. To lift sanctions now would be to run the risk of aborting the process towards the complete eradication of apartheid. Our march to freedom is irreversible. We must not allow fear to stand in our way.

In conclusion, I wish to go to my own words during my trial in 1964. They are as true today as they were then, I quote: "I have fought against white domination and I have fought against black domination. I have cherished the ideal of a democratic and free society in which all persons live together in harmony and with equal opportunity. It is an ideal which I hope to live for and to achieve. But if need be, it is an ideal for which I am prepared to die. Amandla!

OO

Dr. Martin Luther King, Jr.

Civil Rights Leader

Born: 15ᵗʰ January, 1929
Died: 4ᵗʰ April, 1968

Even in the year of 1964, when the world had modernised and got past the era of wars, racial discrimination still existed in the United States. In such times, Dr. Martin Luther King emerged as the leader of the black people and fought for the rights of the blacks. He also advocated non-violence, for which he was often compared to Mahatma Gandhi. King fought for the Civil Rights Act of 1964, and his protests and speeches influenced many, including a large number of whites. He was awarded the 1964 Nobel Prize for Peace. A US national holiday is celebrated in King's honour on the third Monday in January.

On August 28, 1963, King helped to organise the Marchon Washington, an assembly of more than 200,000 protestors. The march was held to pass the Civil Rights Bill that would give the American blacks equal rights. It was here that Dr. Martin Luther King delivered his famous speech, 'I have a dream', expressing his desire of building of a just and equal America.

I Have A Dream

I am happy to join with you today in what will go down in history as the greatest demonstration for freedom in the history of our nation.

Five score years ago, a great American, in whose symbolic shadow, we stand today, signed the Emancipation Proclamation. This momentous decree came as a great beacon, a light of hope to millions of Negro slaves, who had been seared in the flames of withering injustice. It came as a joyous daybreak to end the long night of their captivity.

But 100 years later, the Negro still is not free, the life of the Negro is still sadly crippled by the manacles of segregation and the chains of discrimination. One hundred years later, the Negro lives on a lonely island of poverty in the midst of a vast ocean of material prosperity. One hundred years later, the Negro is still languished in the corners of the American society and finds himself an exile in his own land. And so we've come here today to dramatise a shameful condition.

When the architects of our republic wrote the magnificent words of the Constitution and the Declaration of Independence, they were signing a promissory note to which every American was to fall heir. This note was a promise that all men – yes, black men as well as white men – would be guaranteed the unalienable rights of life, liberty, and the pursuit of happiness.

It is obvious today that America has defaulted on this promissory note insofar as her citizens of colour are concerned. Instead of honouring this sacred obligation, America has given the Negro people a bad check, a check that has come back marked 'insufficient funds'.

But we refuse to believe that the bank of justice is bankrupt. We refuse to believe that there are insufficient funds in the great vaults of opportunity of this nation. And so we've come to cash this check, a check that will give us upon demand the riches of freedom and security of justice. We have also come to his hallowed spot to remind America of the fierce urgency of now. Now is the time to make real the promises of democracy. Now is the time to rise from the dark and desolate valley of segregation to the sunlit path of racial justice. Now is the time to lift our nation from the quicksands of racial injustice to the solid rock of brotherhood. Now is the time to make justice a reality for all of God's children.

This sweltering summer of the Negro's legitimate discontent will not pass until there is an invigorating autumn of freedom and equality. 1963 is not an end but a beginning. There will be neither rest nor tranquillity in America until the Negro is granted his citizenship rights. The whirlwinds of revolt will continue to shake the foundations of our nation until the bright day of justice emerges.

But there is something that I must say to my people, who stand on the warm threshold which leads into the palace of justice. In the process of gaining our rightful place, we must not be guilty of wrongful deeds. Let us not seek to satisfy our thirst for freedom by drinking from the cup of bitterness and hatred. We must forever conduct our struggle on the high plane of dignity and discipline. We must not allow our creative protest to degenerate into physical violence. Again and again, we must rise to the majestic heights of meeting physical force with soul force. The marvellous new militancy which has engulfed the Negro community must not lead us to a distrust of all White people, for many of our White brothers, as evidenced by their presence here today, have come to realise that their destiny is tied up with our destiny. And they have come to realise that their freedom is inextricably bound to our freedom. We cannot walk alone.

And as we walk, we must make the pledge that we shall always march ahead. We cannot turn back. There are those, who are asking the devotees of civil rights, "When will you be satisfied?" We can never be satisfied as long as the Negro is the victim of the unspeakable horrors of police brutality. We can never be satisfied as long as our bodies, heavy with the fatigue of travel, cannot gain lodging in the motels of the highways and the hotels of the cities. We can never be satisfied as long as our children are stripped of their selfhood and robbed of their dignity by signs stating 'for whites only'. We cannot be satisfied as long as a Negro in Mississippi cannot vote and a Negro in New York believes he has nothing for which to vote. No, no we are not satisfied and we will not be satisfied until justice rolls down like waters and righteousness like a mighty stream.

I am not unmindful that some of you have come here out of great trials and tribulations. Some of you have come fresh from narrow jail cells. Some of you have come from areas where your quest for freedom left you battered by storms of persecution and staggered by the winds of police brutality. You have been the veterans of creative suffering. Continue to work with the faith that unearned suffering is redemptive.

Let us not wallow in the valley of despair. I say to you today my friends – so even though we face the difficulties of today and tomorrow, I still have a dream. It is a dream deeply rooted in the American dream.

I have a dream that one day this nation will rise up and live out the true meaning of its creed: "We hold these truths to be self-evident, that all men are created equal."

I have a dream that one day on the red hills of Georgia, the sons of former slaves and the sons of former slave owners will be able to sit down together at the table of brotherhood.

I have a dream that one day even the state of Mississippi, a state sweltering with the heat of injustice, sweltering with the heat of oppression, will be transformed into an oasis of freedom and justice.

I have a dream that my four little children will one day live in a nation where they will not be judged by the colour of their skin but by the content of their character.

I have a dream today.

I have a dream that one day down in Alabama, with its vicious racists, with its governor having his lips dripping with the words of interposition and nullification – one day right there in Alabama, little black boys and black girls will be able to join hands with little white boys and white girls as sisters and brothers.

I have a dream today.

I have a dream that one day every valley shall be exalted, and every hill and mountain shall be made low, the rough places will be made plain, and the crooked places will be made straight, and the glory of the Lord shall be revealed and all flesh shall see it together.

This is our hope. This is the faith that I go back to the South with this faith, we will be able to hew out of the mountain of despair, a stone of hope. With this faith, we will be able to transform the jangling discords of our nation into a beautiful symphony of brotherhood. With this faith, we will be able to work together, to pray together, to struggle together, to go to jail together, to stand up for freedom together, knowing that we will be free one day.

This will be the day, this will be the day when all of God's children will be able to sing with new meaning, "My country 'tis of thee, sweet land of liberty, of thee I sing. Land where my father's died, land of the pilgrim's pride, from every mountainside, let freedom ring!"

Let freedom ring from the snow-capped Rockies of Colorado. Let freedom ring from the curvaceous slopes of California.

But not only that; let freedom ring from Stone Mountain of Georgia.

Let freedom ring from Lookout Mountain of Tennessee.

Let freedom ring from every hill and molehill of Mississippi – from every mountainside.

Let freedom ring. And when this happens, and when we allow freedom ring – when we let it ring from every village and every hamlet, from every state and every city, we will be able to speed up that day when all of God's children – Black men and White men, Jews and Gentiles, Protestants and Catholics – will be able to join hands and sing in the words of the old Negro spiritual: "Free at last! Free at last! Thank God Almighty, we are free at last!"

If we are to be really great people, we must strive in good faith to play a great part in the world. We cannot avoid meeting great issues. All that we can determine for ourselves is whether we shall meet them well or ill. We have a given problem to solve. If we undertake the solution, there is, of course, always danger that we may not solve it aright; but to refuse to undertake the solution simply renders it certain that we cannot possibly solve it aright. No country can long endure if its foundations are not laid deep in the material prosperity which comes from thrift, from business energy and enterprise, from hard, unsparing effort in the fields of industrial activity; but neither was any nation ever yet truly great if it relied upon material prosperity alone. All honour must be paid to the architects of our material prosperity, to the great captains of industry, who have built our factories and our railroads, to the strong men, who toil for wealth with brain or hand; for great is the debt of the nation to these and their kind. But our debt is yet greater to the men whose highest type is to be found in a statesman like Lincoln, a soldier like Grant. They showed by their lives that they recognised the law of work, the law of strife; they toiled to win a competence for themselves and those dependent upon them; but they recognised that there were yet other and even loftier duties – duties to the nation and duties to the race.

The work must be done; we cannot escape our responsibility; and if we are worth our salt, we shall be glad of the chance to do the work – glad of the chance to show ourselves equal to one of the great tasks to set a modern civilisation. But let us not deceive ourselves as to the importance of the task. Let us not be misled by vainglory into underestimating the strain it will put on our powers. Above all, let us, as we value our own self-respect, face the responsibilities with proper seriousness, courage, and high resolve. We must demand the highest order of integrity and ability in our public men, who are to grapple with these new problems.

I preach to you, my countrymen, that our country calls not for the life of ease but for the life of strenuous endeavour.

The twentieth century looms before us big with the fate of many nations. If we stand idly by, if we seek merely swollen, slothful ease and ignoble peace, if we shrink from the hard contests where men must win at hazard of their lives and at the risk of all they hold dear, then the bolder and stronger peoples will pass us by, and will win for themselves the domination of the world. Let us therefore boldly face the life of strife, resolute to do our duty well and manfully; resolute to uphold righteousness by deed and by word; resolute to be both honest and brave, to serve high ideals, yet to use practical methods. Above all, let us shrink from no strife, moral or physical, within or without the nation, provided we are certain that the strife is justified, for it is only through strife, through hard and dangerous endeavour, that we shall ultimately win the goal of true national greatness.

Speeches which
Enlighten the Mind

Theodore Roosevelt

Former President of the United States and a Naturalist

Born: 27th October, 1858
Died: 6th January, 1919

Theodore Roosevelt was the 26th President of the United States, born on October 27, 1858 in New York. He remained President for eight years (1901–09), and in his tenure, he created national forests and laid greater emphasis on conserving mineral, oil, and coal deposits. He also received the Nobel Prize in 1960. He wrote many books on history, politics, travel and nature during his lifetime. He died on January 6, 1919.

On April 10, 1899, Roosevelt delivered a highly inspiring speech, 'The Strenuous Life' to the citizens of the US, admonishing them to live a life of laziness and embrace a life of hard work and perseverance. Roosevelt delivered the speech before the Hamilton Club in Chicago. This everlasting speech still inspires many across the globe.

The Strenuous Life

In speaking to you, men of the greatest city of the West, men of the State which gave to the country Lincoln and Grant, men, who preeminently and distinctly embody all that is most American in the American character, I wish to preach, not the doctrine of ignoble ease, but the doctrine of the strenuous life, the life of toil and effort, of labour and strife; to preach that highest form of success which comes, not to the man, who desires mere easy peace, but to the man, who does not shrink from danger, from hardship, or from bitter toil, and who out of these wins the splendid ultimate triumph.

A life of slothful ease, a life of that peace which springs merely from lack either of desire or of power to strive after great things, is as little worthy of a nation as of an individual. I ask only that what every self-respecting American demands from himself and from his sons shall be demanded of the American nation as a whole. Who among you would teach your boys that ease, that peace, is to be the first consideration in their eyes – to be the ultimate goal after which they strive? You men of Chicago have made this city great, you men of Illinois have done your share, and more than your share, in making America great, because you neither preach nor practise such a doctrine. You work yourselves, and you bring up your sons to work. If you are rich and are worth your salt, you will teach your sons that though they may have leisure, it is not to be spent in idleness; for wisely used leisure merely means that those who possess it, being free from the necessity of working for their livelihood, are all the more bound to carry on some kind of non-remunerative work in science, in letters, in art, in exploration, in historical research – work of the type, we most need in this country, the successful carrying out of which reflects most honour upon the nation. We do not admire the man of timid peace. We admire the man, who embodies victorious effort; the man, who never wrongs his neighbour, who is prompt to help a friend, but who has those virile qualities necessary to win in the stern strife of actual life. It is hard to fail, but it is worse never to have tried to succeed. In this life, we get nothing save by effort. Freedom from effort in the present merely means that there has been stored up effort in the past. A man can be freed from the necessity of work only by the fact that he or his fathers before him have worked to good purpose. If the freedom thus purchased is used aright, and the man still does actual work, though of a different kind, whether as a writer or a general, whether in the field of politics or in the field of exploration and adventure, he shows he deserves his good fortune. But if he treats this period of freedom from the need of actual labour as a period, not of preparation, but of mere enjoyment, even though, perhaps not of vicious enjoyment, he shows that he is simply a cumberer of the earth's surface, and he surely unfits himself to hold his own with his fellows if the need to do so should again arise. A mere life of ease is not in the end a very satisfactory life, and, above all, it is a life which ultimately unfits those, who follow it for serious work in the world.

A healthy state can exist only when the men and women, who make it up lead clean, vigorous, healthy lives; when the children are so trained that they shall endeavour, not to shirk difficulties, but to overcome them; not to seek ease, but to know how to wrest triumph from toil and risk. The man must be glad to do a man's work, to dare and endure and to labour; to keep himself, and to keep those dependent upon him. When men fear work or fear righteous war, when women fear motherhood, they tremble on the brink of doom; and well it is that they should vanish from the earth.

As it is with the individual, so it is with the nation. It is a base untruth to say that happy is the nation that has no history. Thrice happy is the nation that has a glorious history.

Far better it is to dare mighty things, to win glorious triumphs, even though checkered by failure, than to take rank with those poor spirits, who neither enjoy much nor suffer much, because they live in the gray twilight that knows not victory nor defeat.

Thank God for the iron in the blood of our fathers, the men, who upheld the wisdom of Lincoln, and bore sword or rifle in the armies of Grant! Let us, the children of the men who proved themselves equal to the mighty days, let us, the children of the men, who carried the great Civil War to a triumphant conclusion, praise the God of our fathers that the ignoble counsels of peace were rejected; that the suffering and loss, the blackness of sorrow and despair, were unflinchingly faced, and the years of strife endured.

Swami Vivekananda

A Renowned Spiritual Leader

Born: 12ᵗʰ January, 1863
Died: 4ᵗʰ July, 1902

Born as Narendranath Datta on January 12, 1863, Swami Vivekananda went on to become the most renowned and respected spiritual leader of India. He was a disciple of a famous teacher, Ramakrishna. He gained knowledge by reading Vedas and spread its values in western countries, where he gained immense respect. Unfortunately for the nation, Swami Vivekananda died at a young age of 39 in 1902.

On September 11, 1893, Swami Vivekananda addressed the World Parliament of Religions at Chicago. It was here that his teachings became famous. He spoke of the Indian teachings of those of Bhagavad Gita, peace and end of violence in the world. He was widely applauded for his rich speech by many famous spiritual leaders and elite guests. Coming to India after four years of travelling in America and Europe, he delivered the speech, 'A message of hope' at Rameshwaram, urging people to embrace hope and hard work. This speech still invigorates the feeling of nationalism amongst Indians worldwide.

At the World Parliament of Religions

Sisters and Brothers of America!

It fills my heart with joy unspeakable to rise in response to the warm and cordial welcome which you have given us.

I thank you in the name of the most ancient order of monks in the world; I thank you in the name of the mother of religions, and I thank you in the name of millions and millions of Hindu people of all classes and sects.

I am proud to belong to a religion which has taught the world both tolerance and universal acceptance. We believe not only in universal toleration, but we accept all religions as true. I am proud to belong to a nation which has sheltered the refugees of all religions and all nations of the earth. I am proud to tell you that we have gathered in our bosom the purest remnant of the Israelites, who came to Southern India and took refuge with us in the very year in which their holy temple was shattered to pieces by Roman tyranny. I am proud to belong to the religion which has sheltered and is still fostering the remnant of the grand Zoroastrian nation. I will quote to you, brethren, a few lines from a hymn which I remember to have repeated from my earliest boyhood, which is everyday repeated by millions of human beings: "As the different streams having their sources in different paths which men take through different tendencies, various though they appear, crooked or straight, all lead to YOU."

The present convention is in itself a declaration to the world of the wonderful doctrine preached in the Bhagavad-Gita: "Whosoever comes to Me, through whatsoever form, I reach him; all men are struggling through paths which in the end lead to me."

Sectarianism, bigotry, and its horrible descendant, fanaticism, have long possessed this beautiful earth. They have filled the earth with violence, drenched it often and often with human blood, destroyed civilisations and sent whole nations to despair. Had it not been for these horrible demons, human society would be far more advanced than it is now. But their time has come; and I hope that the bell that tolled this morning in honour of this convention may be the death-knell of all fanaticism, of all persecutions with the sword or with the pen, and of all uncharitable feelings between persons wending their way to the same goal.

A Message of Hope

Great works are to be done, wonderful powers have to be worked out., we have to teach other nations many things. India is the motherland of philosophy, spirituality, ethics, sweetness, gentleness and love. India is still the first and foremost of all the nations of the world in these respects. I have heard it being said that our masses are slow, that they do not want any education, and that they do not care for any information. I, too, at one time had an absurd leaning towards that opinion myself, but I find experience is a far more glorious teacher than any amount of speculation, or any amount of books written by globetrotters and hasty observers. This experience teaches me that they are not dense, that they are not slow, but they as eager and thirsty for information as any other race under the sun. Each nation has its own part to play, and naturally, its own peculiarity and individuality with which its born. Each represents, as it were, one peculiar note in harmony of nations, and this is its very life, its vitality. In it is the backbone, the foundation, and the bedrock of national life. In this blessed land, the foundation, the backbone, the life-centre is religion and religion alone.

Talk to the Hindu mind on spirituality, religion, God, soul, the Infinite, or spiritual freedom, and I assure you, the lowest peasant in India is better informed on these subjects than many a so-called philosopher in other lands. The nation still lives because it still holds God, to the treasure-house of religion and spirituality.

Learn good knowledge with all devotion from the lowest caste. Learn the way to freedom, even if it comes from a *pariah*, by serving him. If a woman is a jewel, take her in marriage even if she comes from a low family of the lowest caste. Stand on your feet, and assimilate what you can; learn from every nation, take what is of use to you. Each man has a mission in life, which is the result of all his past *karma*. Each of you was born with a splendid heritage, which is past of your glorious nation. Millions of your ancestors are watching, as it were every action of yours, so be alert. Mark my words, if you give up that spirituality, leaving it aside to go after the materialistic western civilisation, the result will be that in three generations, your race will be extinct. The backbone of the nation will be broken, the foundation upon which the national edifice has been built will be undermined, and the result will be annihilation all around.

Therefore, my friends, the way out is that first and foremost, we must keep firm hold on spirituality – that gift handed to us by our glorious ancestors. Let us work hard, my brothers, this is no time to sleep. She is there ready waiting. She is only sleeping. Arise and awake and see her seated here on her eternal throne, rejuvenated, more glorious that she ever was – this motherland of ours.

OO

Socrates

A Famous Greek Philosopher

Born: 470 B.C.

Died: 399 B.C.

Socrates was born in 470 B.C. and lived in Greece, the nation that produced many great thinkers and philosophers in the ancient world, and it would not be wrong to say that Socrates was the greatest of them. Socrates greatly influenced the youth of Athens by engaging them in philosophical conversations. The administration blamed Socrates for misguiding the youth of the nation, and sentenced him to death in 399 B.C. His death sentence is often criticised in the modern world.

When the judges sentenced him to death, Socrates did not argue with them, and delivered a moving speech, 'Apology' to Athenians. In his speech, he did not defend himself but told about his life and commitments of life. The speech 'Apology' was written later by his famous student, Plato.

Apology

O Athenians, I will begin at the beginning, and ask what is the accusation which has given rise to the slander of my person, and in fact, has encouraged this charge against me, Well, what do the slanderers say? They shall be my prosecution and I will sum up their words in an affidavit: 'Socrates is an evil-doer, and a curious person, who searches into things under the earth and in heaven, and he makes the worse appear the better cause; and he teaches the aforesaid doctrines to others.' Such is the nature of the accusation: it is just what you have yourselves seen in the comedy of Aristophanes, who has introduced a man whom he calls Socrates going about and saying that he walks in air and talking a deal of nonsense concerning matters of which I do not pretend to know either much or little, not that I mean to speak disparagingly of anyone, who is a student of natural philosophy. But the simple truth is, O Athenians, that I have nothing to do with physical speculations: many of those here present are witnesses to the truth of this.

As little foundation is there for the report that I am a teacher, and take money; this accusation has no more truth in it than the other. Although, if a man were really able to instruct mankind, to receive money for giving instruction would, in my opinion, be an honour to him. I dare say, Athenians, that someone among you will say, 'Socrates, but what is the origin of these accusations which are brought against you; there must have been something strange which you have been doing? All these rumours and this talk about you would never have arisen if you had been like other men: tell us, then, what is the cause of them, for we should be sorry to judge hastily of you.' Now I regard this as a fair challenge, and I will endeavour to explain to you the reason why I am called wise and have such an evil fame. And although some of you may think that I am joking, I declare that I will tell you the entire truth. Men of Athens, this reputation of mine has come of a certain sort of wisdom which I possess. If you ask me what kind of wisdom, I reply, wisdom such as may perhaps be attained by every man, for to that extent I am inclined to believe that I am wise;

whereas the persons of whom, I was speaking have a superhuman wisdom, which I may fail to describe, because I have it not myself; and he, who says that I have, speaks falsely, and is taking away my character.

There is another thing: young men of the richer classes, who have not much to do, come about me of their own accord; they like to hear the pretenders examined, and they often imitate me, and proceed to examine others; there are plenty of persons, as they quickly discover, who think that they know something, but really know little or nothing; and then those, who are examined by them, instead of being angry with themselves are angry with me: this confounded Socrates, they say; this villainous misleader of youth!, and then if somebody asks them, Why, what evil does he practise or teach?, they do not know, and can't tell; but in order that they may not appear to be at a loss, they repeat the readymade charges which are used against all philosophers about teaching things up in the clouds and under the earth, and making the worse appear the better cause; for they do not like to confess that their pretence of knowledge has been detected, which is the truth; and as they are numerous and ambitious and energetic, and are drawn up in battle array and have persuasive tongues, they have filled your ears with their loud and inveterate calumnies. And this is the reason, why my accusers have set upon me. And this, O men of Athens, is the truth and the whole truth; I have concealed nothing, I have dissembled nothing. And yet, I know that my plainness of speech makes them hate me, and what is their hatred but a proof that I am speaking the truth? Hence, has arisen the prejudice against me.

Someone will say: And are you not ashamed, Socrates, of a course of life which is likely to bring you to an untimely end? To him I may fairly answer: There you are mistaken: a man, who is good for anything ought not to calculate the chance of living or dying; he ought only to consider whether in doing anything he is doing right or wrong, acting the part of a good man or of a bad. Whereas, upon your view, the heroes, who fell at Troy were not good for much, and the son of Thetis above all, who altogether despised danger in comparison with disgrace; and when he was so eager to slay Hector, his goddess mother said to him, that if he avenged his companion Patroclus, and slew Hector, he would die himself, 'Fate,' she said, in these or the like words, 'waits for you next after Hector;' he, receiving this warning, utterly despised danger and death, and instead of fearing them, feared rather to live in dishonour, and not to avenge his friend. 'Let me die forthwith,' he replies, 'and be avenged of my enemy, rather than abide here by the beaked ships, a laughing-stock and a burden of the earth.' Had Achilles any thought of death and danger? For wherever a man's place is, whether the place which he has chosen or that in which he has been placed by a commander, there he ought to remain in the hour of danger; he should not think of death or of anything but of disgrace. And this, O men of Athens, is a true saying.

Men of Athens, I honour and love you; but I shall obey God rather than you, and while I have life and strength, I shall never cease from the practice and teaching of philosophy, exhorting anyone whom I meet and saying to him after my manner: You, my friend, a citizen of the great and mighty and wise city of Athens, are you not ashamed of heaping up the greatest amount of money and honour and reputation, and caring so little about wisdom and truth and the greatest improvement of the soul, which you never regard or heed at all? And if the person with whom I am arguing, says: Yes, but I do care; then I do not leave him or let him go at once; but I proceed to interrogate and examine and cross-examine him, and if I think that he has no virtue in him, but only says that he has, I reproach him with undervaluing the greater, and overvaluing the less. And I shall repeat the same words to everyone whom I meet, young and old, citizen and alien, but especially to the citizens, in as much as they are my brethren. For know that this is the command necessity of God; and I believe that no greater good has ever happened in the state than my service to the God. For I do nothing but go about persuading you all, old and young alike, not to take thought for your persons or your properties, but first and chiefly to care about the greatest improvement of the soul. I tell you that virtue is not given by money, but that from virtue comes money and every other good of man, public as well as private. This is my teaching, and if this is the doctrine which corrupts the youth, I am a mischievous person. But if anyone says that this is not my teaching, he is speaking an untruth.

Someone may wonder why I go about in private giving advice and busying myself with the concerns of others, but do not venture to come forward in public and advise the state. I will tell you why. You have heard me speak at sundry times and in diverse places of an oracle or sign which comes to me, and is the divinity which accusers ridicule in the indictment. This sign, which is a kind of voice, first began to come to me when I was a child; it always forbids but never commands me to do anything which I am going to do. This is what deters me from being a politician. And rightly, as I think. For I am certain, O men of Athens, that if I had engaged in politics, I should have perished long ago, and done no good either to you or to myself. And do not be offended at my telling you the truth: for the truth is, that no man, who goes to war with you or any other multitude, honestly striving against the many lawless and unrighteous deeds which are done in a state, will save his life; he who will fight for the right, if he would live even for a brief space, must have a private station and not a public one.

Well, Athenians, this and the like of this is all the defence which I have to offer. Yet one word more. Perhaps, there may be someone who is offended at me, when he calls to mind how he himself on a similar, or even a less serious occasion, prayed and entreated the judges with many tears, and how he produced his children in court, which was a moving spectacle, together with a host of relations and friends; whereas I, who am probably in danger of my life, will do none of these things. The contrast may occur to his mind, and he may be set against me, and vote in anger because he is displeased at me on this account.

But, setting aside the question of public opinion, there seems to be something wrong in asking a favour of a judge, and thus procuring an acquittal, instead of informing and convincing him. For his duty is, not to make a present of justice, but to give judgement; and he has sworn that he will judge according to the laws, and not according to his own good and pleasure; and we ought not to encourage you, nor should you allow yourselves to be encouraged, in this habit of perjury, there can be no piety in that. For if, O men of Athens, by force of persuasion and entreaty, I could overpower your oaths, then I should be teaching you to believe that there are no gods, and in defending should simply convict myself of the charge of not believing in them. But that is not so, far otherwise. For I do believe that there are gods, and in a sense higher than that in which any of my accusers believe in them. And to you and to God I commit my cause, to be determined by you as is best for you and me.

Let us reflect on death, and we shall see that there is great reason to hope that death is good; for one of two things, either death is a state of nothingness and utter unconsciousness, or, as men say, there is a change and migration of the soul from this world to another. Now if you suppose that there is no consciousness, but a sleep like the sleep of him, who is undisturbed even by dreams, death will be an unspeakable gain. For if a person were to select the night in which his sleep was undisturbed even by dreams, and were to compare with this the other days and nights of his life, and then were to tell us how many days and nights he had passed in the course of his life better and more pleasantly than this one, I think that any man but the greatest king will not find many such days or nights, when compared to the others. Now if death be of such a nature, I say that to die is gain. But if death is the journey to another place, and there, as men say, all the dead abide, what good, O my friends and judges, can be greater than this? What would not a man give if he might converse with Orpheus and Musaeus and Hesiod and Homer? Nay, if this be true, let me die again and again!

Wherefore, O judges, be of good cheer about death, and know of a certainty, that no evil can happen to a good man, either in life or after death. He and his are not neglected by the gods; nor has my own approaching end happened by mere chance. But I see clearly that the time had arrived when it was better for me to die and be released from trouble. . .

The hour of departure has arrived, and we go our separate ways, I to die, and you to live. Which of these two is better, only God knows.

William Lyon Phelps

American Educator, Literary Critic and Author

Born: 1865
Died: 1943

William Lyon Phelps, born in 1865, was an American educator, literary critic and author. He served as a professor of English at Yale University from 1901 to 1933. He was a popular orator amongst the masses. His preaches in church became so popular that the church had to be expanded twice to accommodate people! He also possessed a personal library of over six thousand books!

In one of his famous speeches, he talked of the significance of books. This speech was delivered on April 6, 1933 in which he described books as eternal treasure that provides immense knowledge and wisdom.

The Pleasure of Books

The habit of reading is one of the greatest resources of mankind and we enjoy reading books that belong to us much more than if they are borrowed. A borrowed book is like a guest in the house. It must be treated with punctiliousness, with a certain considerate formality. You must see that it sustains no damage; it must not suffer while under your roof. You cannot leave it carelessly, you cannot mark it, you cannot turn down the pages, you cannot use it familiarly. And then, some day, although this is seldom done, you really ought to return it.

But your own books belong to you; you treat them with that affectionate intimacy that annihilates formality. Books are for use, not for show. You should own no book that you are afraid to mark up, or afraid to place on the table, wide open and face down. A good reason for marking favourite passages in books is that this practice enables you to remember more easily the significant sayings, to refer to them quickly, and then in later years, it is like visiting a forest where you once blazed a trail. You have the pleasure of going over the old ground, and recalling both the intellectual scenery and your own earlier self.

Everyone should begin collecting a private library in youth. The instinct of private property, which is fundamental in human beings, can here be cultivated with every advantage and no evils. One should have one's own bookshelves, which should not have doors, glass windows, or keys; they should be free and accessible to the hand as well as to the eye. The best of mural decorations is books – they are more varied in colour and appearance than any wallpaper, they are more attractive in design, and they have the prime advantage of being separate personalities, so that if you sit alone in the room in the firelight, you are surrounded with intimate friends. The knowledge that they are there in plain view is both stimulating and refreshing. You do not have to read them all. Most of my indoor life is spent in a room containing six thousand books, and I have a stock answer to the invariable question that comes from strangers. "Have you read all of these books?" "Some of them twice." This reply is both true and unexpected.

There are of course no friends like living, breathing, corporeal men and women. My devotion to reading has never made me a recluse. How could it? Books are of the people, by the people, for the people. Literature is the immortal part of history. It is the best and most enduring part of personality. But book-friends have this advantage over living friends; you can enjoy the most truly aristocratic society in the world whenever you want it.

In a private library, you can at any moment converse with Socrates or Shakespeare or Carlyle or Dumas or Dickens or Shaw or Barrie. And there is no doubt that in these books you see these men at their best. They wrote for *you*. They 'laid themselves out', they did their ultimate best to entertain you, to make a favourable impression. You are necessary to them as an audience is to an actor; only instead of seeing them masked, you look into their innermost heart of heart.

The World's Greatest
Seers & Philosophers

Amidst modern stress, strife and terrorism, it is imperative to realise what God is really all about. Nothing achieves this objective better than reading about the lives and teachings of the world's greatest seers and philosophers.

Although dealing with metaphysics, the focus of this book is spiritual rather than religious. For spirituality speaks only the language of love, compassion, oneness and bliss. Whatever you may wish to call the Ultimate Reality–God, Brahman, Cosmic Consciousness, Atman–the first-hand experiences and writings of the great seers and philosophers brings home the Truth that every seeker longs for.

Demy size • Pages: 142 • Price: Rs. 80/- • Postage: Rs. 15/-

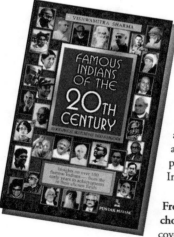

Famous Indians of the
20th Century

For people of all age groups, reading about the lives and times of great Indians is always inspiring and uplifting. This book presents insights on more than 100 famous Indians of the 20th century.

From their early years to achievements in the chosen fields, *Famous Indians of the 20th Century* covers all the relevant details. The book makes excellent reading for students, teachers, parents and all other professionals seeking credible information on the lives and achievements of famous Indians of the 20th century.

Demy size • Pages: 224 • Price: Rs. 80/- • Postage: Rs. 15/-